Praise for *More ABCs of Parenting*

'As the mother of a young adolescent, reading Gouri's book is like living a day in my life. Her book, outlining practical and real solutions to problems and how to deal with the myriad issues that arise in bringing up a child in today's world, makes for a unique companion to parents of today. *More ABCs of Parenting* is a must-have for every parent of today'—**Dr Usha BalaKrishnan** (Active PTA member, Jamnabai School, and museum expert)

'This book, just like the previous *ABCs of Parenting*, contains useful common sense tips for parents who need some hand holding at times, and who want suggestions for appropriate intervention in everyday situations. Gouri's easy-to-read style and the identifiable situations she discusses will make *More ABCs of Parenting* a friendly companion for every parent'—**Prof Dr Minnu Bhonsle** (PhD Consulting Psychotherapist Trainer in Client-Centred Therapy & REBT)

'*More ABCs of Parenting* brings wonderfully sensible parenting suggestions through case studies that look at common dilemmas that modern parents and children face today. Gouri Dange's style is informal, empathetic, thought-provoking and of abiding value. Will be of interest to any parent looking for ways of bringing up well balanced children' —**Dr Dayal Mirchandani** (Psychiatrist)

'Gouri, in *More ABCs of Parenting*, has shown the way to a lot of new-age parents like me who have to deal with issues which weren't relevant in our parents' times. I, as a parent, am always in a bind about whose advice to follow and what is the right way to bring up children today. Parenting, apart from being exhilarating, is also

difficult, demanding, and scary. Gouri has given an exhaustive list of solutions in a very reassuring, comforting manner yet with a firm hand. Somewhat like what a good parent should be. I absolutely loved the tone of the book and I know I have a new ally in my parenting journey in the form of Gouri's *More ABCs of Parenting*'
—**Renuka Shahane** (TV and theatre actor)

'Gouri Dange's sane voice never condescends or patronises to young parents as her warm, wise, insightful and practicable advice is delivered. She addresses contemporary parenting challenges with her trademark dry wit, dealing with real issues the young Indian family faces like absentee parents, alcohol, bigotry, mother tongues, gender stereotyping and sex education to name just a few'
—**Smriti Lamech** (Journalist, blogger)

'This is not just a book on parenting. Gouri Dange has written a book telling us how to live. She talks about serious subjects like the effects of parents' marital discord on children, on important subjects like behaviour towards domestic staff. A truly well-written book'
—**Dr Manasee Palshikar**

'Gouri's book is an elegant string of beautiful pearls, simple but not simplistic. Her tips on parenting are both delightful and incisive, a distillate of her own innate wisdom and experience. To parents, this is of course a godsend but to those yet to embark on that wonderful journey, it is inspiration to be one (it certainly was for me, making me somewhat wistful!)'—**Dr Tarun Israni** (Consultant psychiatrist and psychotherapist)

MORE **ABCs**
OF
PARENTING

MORE ABCs
OF
PARENTING

GOURI DANGE

RANDOM HOUSE INDIA

Published by Random House India in 2013

1

Copyright © Gouri Dange 2013

Random House Publishers India Private Limited
Windsor IT Park, 7th Floor
Tower-B, A-1, Sector-125
Noida 201301, UP

Random House Group Limited
20 Vauxhall Bridge Road
London SW1V 2SA
United Kingdom

978 81 8400 310 9

Typeset in Adobe Garamond Pro by R. Ajith Kumar

Printed and bound in India by Replika Press Private Limited

For Kimaya and Niharika—new chapters in my life

Contents

Foreword

Parenting is an art, but unlike other art forms which one chooses, learns and hopes to master, parenting is that art form which one has thrust upon them and is expected to master! In my three decades of experience of observing parents and their children visiting my clinic, raising my own two, who are in their late twenties and pitching in parenting my nieces and nephews, I have realized that just as every parent comes with their special skill set, each child comes with their own fingerprints of challenges. Yet parenting is probably the most gratifying of relationships. When one contributes a well rounded individual into the swirling pool that we call society, it is not a job well done but well finished!

For those of us who have read Gouri Dange's *ABCs of Parenting;* written in her engaging style, that book to borrow the author's own term, is a primer, a preparatory coat, which has guided many parents in an affectionate way. ABC stood for Apologies, Boundaries, Criticism. I have seen many a parent quickly flipping to see if what they wanted was rightfully represented by the alphabet. Often they said, 'Ah it's there', but at times they wished for more.

More ABCs of Parenting will be much appreciated, as it is multi-layered, intense, and case based. It deals with a whole gamut of situations faced by today's parents, who are hard pressed for time and suffer from dipping energy levels. Besides being a wonderful read, it has a set of dos and donts after every chapter.

Dr Barnali Bhattacharya
April 2013

Introduction

The first time I met a counsellor was in the seventh grade, in the Singapore American School in the 1970s. The early years of that decade were marked by student protests in many parts of the world, drugs and alcohol, rock 'n' roll, teen sex, and so many other things that parents and teachers were suddenly grappling with. The school felt that every student needed to meet the counsellor regularly so that they got a sense of what was going on inside our heads! The word quickly went around the class and we assumed that a counsellor was some sort of an interrogator—a kind smiling one, but an interrogator nevertheless!

However, when I finally sat across the table to Mrs Minelli and Mr Baker, I found myself drawn out, and was able to talk about my adolescent angst, everything from battles with my mother, to an unrequited crush, and on to fears about failing in physics! It slowly became clear to all of us kids, and of course to the school, that while the larger picture of 'societal evils of the era' was what they were worried about, our child minds had questions, worries, and fears that were universal and timeless and needed a listening ear. Something that every generation of kids face even if the externals and the details may differ from decade to decade.

When I think back about how that pair of counsellors could draw me, and each one of us, out of our shells and offer suggestions, calm our feverish imaginations at times, and help us connect to our better selves, I now know that I was in the presence of two people who 'spoke so that children listened and listened so that children spoke'!

For me, this is the mark of a good counsellor and the proof that counselling, of both kids and adults, individuals and families, is indeed much more than simply brushing away people's fears and telling them to get on with it! In training and then practising as a family counsellor, I have learnt that people cannot be 'told' what to do. What a counsellor can do is to show people how to be authentic and true to themselves. Counsellors also teach us to honestly work on those aspects of our behaviour that is simply not serving us well.

When I work with parents, I am always so impressed with people who 'want to get it right'. They are not people who want to 'be right', they want to get it right, which means they want to become true enablers of their children's growth.

The 21st century brings with it its own pressures on parenting—right from wondering whether to become a parent at all, to wondering if you are simply failing as a parent every day! Technology, distance, speed, and networks have brought the world closer, but perhaps taken families further away from each other. Sudden wealth in relatively young urban families, a blitz of products to choose from, and towering aspirations have all ended up giving us many lifestyle skills, while quietly robbing us of life skills.

It is in this framework that parents exist, willy-nilly. Children are maturing earlier, and the elderly and experienced in our families have suddenly become irrelevant, or we have made them so. It is in this context that many aspects of parenting now need 'outside' aid, be it from counsellors, or workshops, or books on parenting.

More ABCs of Parenting is one such aid. Based on the questions that crop up time and again in my counselling clinic, and in the long-running Q & A column that I write for the weekend supplement, *Lounge* in the daily paper *Mint*, I have made a selection of parenting topics. The topics for this book take into account the everyday exigencies as also the more nuanced needs of both parents and children.

As the smaller and larger issues surrounding the nurture of our young ones come up, parents feel at times that they have been thrown into the deep end, with little preparation, and commanded: Now Swim! In the first *ABCs of Parenting*, I touched upon a range of valuable and essential parenting skills, ranging from A for Apologies right up to Z for Zombies. In *More ABCs of Parenting*, you will find new skill sets to pick up, to help you in the joyous, exhilarating and yes, sometimes very demanding but always fulfilling journey of being a parent. This book does not offer black-and-white, one size fits all solutions. Rather, it takes a nuanced, empathetic look at the contemporary issues that parents face. With the help of real-life cases, *More ABCs of Parenting* provides you a walk-through of a host of likely parenting situations and scenarios, and offers useful insights and counsel. The gentle lessons in this book help parents set their priorities, re-look at their strategies, and take confident steps forward to be genuinely and authentically present in their children's lives.

The book gently urges parents to look inwards for answers and to understand themselves better so that the responsibility of parenting becomes an exploration, a learning experience, and the adventure of a lifetime.

A for

Absent Parent

Children can become aggressive and resentful when they do not get enough of their parents. Parents, on the other hand, justify being away for long stretches because they have to keep the financial benefits of the family in mind. However, this often turns counter-productive and affects the parent–child relationship.

Thirteen-year-old Kartik has become withdrawn and uncommunicative with his dad. For the last couple of years, his dad has been in a job that involves a lot of travelling. This means he is home for only around six days a month. He looks forward to bond with his son when he comes home but to his frustration, his son seems to not want much to do with him during these days.

Sometimes Kartik outbursts against his father in front of his mother. The issues are usually minor like 'why did he talk and laugh so loudly in that restaurant?', or 'why does he have to come for Open Day at school when he doesn't even know what's going on in my school life?', etc. His mother is bewildered at this hostility and cannot understand what makes Kartik so angry. She has tried explaining to him that though Dad may not be present, he is in touch with her daily and knows what school issues come up, etc. But Kartik remains angry and withdrawn from his father.

Now the father begins to feel alienated and ignored by his son, and begins to feel depressed. A close family friend advises him to leave his travelling job and take up something in the city so that he can be with the family on a daily basis. However, these are his prime professional years, and after all, it's all for his family's future that he has taken up a job that pays well, he reasons. This is a dilemma faced by many families. So what is the way forward?

No doubt, some part of Kartik's outbursts can be attributed to the phase of life that he is in—adolescent boys do feel animosity towards their fathers, and can become hyper-critical during this time. However, it is equally true that a largely absent father is not a good idea at all for a growing boy. Yes, today people have to go wherever their work takes them to become better achievers, but perhaps we need to step back, as parents and householders, and make our own clear assessment of what the trade-off is. Particularly in a situation where the parents can see that their absence is affecting the kids. After all, the message is quite clear from Kartik: that he needs more than just a breadwinner for a father. And as that need is not being fulfilled, he is turning his need for his father and frustration at his absence into a 'who wants him here anyway' kind of counter rejection.

Sadly, most tired, overworked, absent parents tell themselves 'But I'm doing this for the kids.' It's true that some of our career pursuits are to do with giving our kids good things, vacations, exposure, and access to paid Western education when they grow older. However, as we can see in the case of Kartik and so many kids around us, children are hungry for more than just gifts; even if they are happy to have those, they yearn for their parent's presence.

Psychiatrists' couches and counselling rooms are overflowing with men and women whose dads were too busy, too ill-equipped, or too unthinking to be parents who were genuinely present in their children's lives. Rarely are these places, the clinics and couches, filled with people whose fathers and mothers couldn't provide them with bright and shiny things, allowances, and a fully-paid Western education!

Kartik's parents tried to get the help of a counsellor to 'fix' the problem. But in this situation, it is pointless to say—'the career choice we have made is not negotiable, and now let us find a way to fix the problem with the child'. Our choices impact our child's everyday world and his larger emotional universe too. There is really no getting away from that. Any 'behavioural' 'surface' changes that you bring to the situation can at best be tinkering with the problem.

So here's what parents in this situation would need to see through and prioritize by asking themselves:

How much of our pursuits of the big bucks are really in pursuit of a big lifestyle and big career strokes?

Once we have the answer to this, it will be easy to readjust our choices to become more present in our kids' lives. It may mean letting go of various very tempting 'opportunities', but doing it with a certain amount of self-awareness—'I would have liked to do that, but the cost-to-family will be too high.' Companies talk about 'cost-to-company' when they offer you a job, as parents, we must take into account 'cost-to-family' when we consider these offers.

We are not talking about suddenly living the life of ascetics and yogis. We are talking about not turning parenting and earning into two mutually exclusive activities.

Dos and Don'ts

- If and when we do choose to cut back on earnings and be more present in our childrens' lives, be careful not to remind your child about it or rub it in to the child's mind.

- Some parents end up saying things like 'Papa is getting paid less so that he can be with you. And that's why we can't go on a scuba-diving vacation', or 'You better work hard and get a scholarship because your father doesn't earn in dollars anymore, and can't afford to send you abroad.' Statements such as these defeat the purpose completely. It brings in a great degree of joylessness, and also throws in a garnishing of guilt on to your child's plate.

- These 'trade-offs' are for us as parents to make and reconcile/readjust ourselves to. They aren't to be held over your childrens' heads as shining examples of our sacrifices and good parenting choices.

Adopted

Adopted children can behave in a resentful and unreasonable manner as they approach adolescence. Be sensitive to his/her confusions and emotions, but do not feel compelled to keep proving yourself as a 'real' parent

Amir is an adopted child of eleven years. He has been told about it by his parents when he was five. The younger child in the family is his adoptive parents' biological daughter, who is seven. Amir's parents have been pained and worried to hear their son making negative references to being adopted. He has always known it, and up to now had no real deep-rooted issues with his parents. However, he now ascribes many of their disciplinary restrictions—and they are the normal ones that would apply to both children—to his being adopted. He has recently said it out loud even in front of guests, which makes things very awkward. Ina, their daughter, has just the opposite to say—that her parents are partial and kinder to him because he is adopted. The parents are hard-pressed to prove to their kids that there is no such bias operating.

It seems like there are two issues involved here. One is that Amir is entering an age—adolescence—where his earlier ease or innocence about the fact that he is adopted is now being replaced with some kind of anxiety and doubts about his 'place' in the scheme of life. Up until now, while he was still his parents' little boy, his being adopted was only a vague concept, and his sense of well-being was not challenged, because he related himself to his parents as his nurturers. Now, and this is natural with all kids his age, his emotions and experiences are developing and he is forming an identity for himself, separate from that of his parents, with uncertainty and questions beginning to arise. This happens with all kids, adopted or biological. With adopted children, the inevitable question about the circumstances surrounding why they were given up for adoption by their biological parents is bound to come up and the child is going to ask this, and a parent is going to have to deal sensitively with it: when you talk to an adopted child with another sibling, like Amir and Ira, who is directing anger and resentment towards you, you can also re-iterate this by saying you brought him home because he was precious to you from the time that you set eyes on him (or similar words) and also had the other child because he needs a sibling, someone to love and grow up with too!

However, the other issue here is that children do tend to manipulate parents on sensitive issues. In Amir's case, it is the fact of being adopted; other kids find something else to hold over their parents' heads. It's all part of the 'ammo' in a budding adolescent's armoury. He has obviously touched a raw nerve by saying this to his parents, and this kind of allegation neatly derails the issue at hand—his disciplining. The topic shifts to whether he is loved or not, and that his parents motives for disciplining him are to do with the fact that he's adopted. There you have it, a neat little side-step tool that he has used to great effect. The biological daughter too is 'using' the word adopted to voice her own complaints and anger about perceived injustices. Perhaps it is time to stop taking on these allegations so seriously.

Dos and Don'ts

- The parents can sit down with the children, and tell them that this 'because I am adopted' 'because he is adopted' phrase is going to be put into cold storage and that it will not be used in future.
- Of course, we need to continue to sensitively help a child with emotional issues and answer questions about his adoption. It is just when you feel that there is almost a glib and convenient use of this fact by kids that you should firmly refuse to get drawn into the subject.

Aggression

Bullying behaviour can be corrected if parents get to the root of the problem. Why is your child resorting to supercilious behaviour? What does his sense of worth hinge on? Is he picking up cues from your own family interactions?

Abha and Sanjay are shocked and worried. They have been told by several other parents that their twelve-year-old Salil is bullying other kids. He has not punched anyone, but he threatens the other kids in school and shoves them around when forming teams or while playing. He also uses very aggressive language, but not swear words. When his parents try to talk to him he says, 'The other kids are stupid and won't listen to me and are sissies.' Then one day, he got punched by a girl who got sick of him bossing them around. This was a total meltdown point for him and he now refuses to go out to play at all. What do parents do in a situation such as this?

In a way, this is a good time for the parents to try to step in gently. The girl punching him has done half the job in a way, which is to give him the message that a) bullies are at first feared, but soon they get their comeuppance and are rendered powerless and b) bullying has an extremely limited shelf life. Which is not to say that we need to gloat or laugh at Salil or say 'serves you right', etc. What is important is that the parents can now use this opportunity to talk to him about how relationships with friends, team-mates, school friends, siblings, and cousins can and should never be about power. This is the time to show him some of the joys and benefits of co-operation.

Once you get a bullying child to talk, find out where his or her dismissive attitude ('they're all stupid and sissies') has emerged from. This way you can also find out if he is trying to feel superior to them all (based usually on a feeling of inadequacy) or whether he is genuinely ahead of them in terms of thinking, planning and strategizing (all of which comes into play with team games) and is frustrated by their unwillingness to see it his way. Whatever a parent finds out, they have their work cut out for them accordingly. If it is a matter of him wanting to feel superior and supercilious, you need to find out why his self worth hinges on this. Simultaneously, reflect on your own family interactions, attitudes and conversations—is there power play, dismissive talk, and passive aggression at work in some form at home? In your interactions with each other as adults and with your son, or any other significant elders' interactions with the child, are there subtle pressure tactics that are being used?

If you find that this is not at play, and what is happening is the latter scenario, where he is frustrated by the 'noncompliance' with his good ideas, then first help him change his ways of communicating them. He simply has to learn non-physical and non-hostile ways of putting his ideas across. That is the hallmark of all leaders, isn't it—they have great ideas, and know how to communicate and execute them without using force of any kind—verbal or physical. Here you can build on your child's qualities and talents by encouraging him to get involved in social activities (such as clubs, music lessons, non-violent sports, nature-based outings). Which does not mean that you pluck him out of playing with the neighbourhood kids and send him to the rarified atmosphere of some other activity alone. I suggest you have him do both.

If in the process of getting to the root of a child's aggressive behaviour, you uncover unhealthy family behaviour patterns, it's important to consider seeing a counsellor, who would neutrally and compassionately get all of the family past this phase. While there is no need to be alarmed and anxious, do take your child's bullying behaviour seriously and tackle it systematically at a personal and family level.

Many aggressive children are looking for attention, and even negative attention will do.

Dos and Don'ts

- Parents should spend some quiet time with an aggressive child, every day if possible—either during meal times, post-bathing, before bedtime, or any other time that is convenient for both you and your child.

Alcohol

Social drinking, responsibly handled within the family, need not cause undue anxiety about its negative effect on children. Yet, parents need to be cautious about keeping children out of that space.

Saurav's family has had a few alcoholics in it. His wife's family drinks socially, they enjoy their drinks or beer at parties, etc. However, Saurav is anxious that his sons, aged thirteen and eleven, may get drawn into drinking because of its presence in all social occasions and because of the genetic background from his side.

We all have a relationship with alcohol, whether we drink or abstain, drink in moderation or excessively, take the phenomenon in our stride or see drinking as a big evil. I understand Saurav's anxiety on the issue, given his family background. In households where there is responsible, social drinking, as it seems to be in Saurav's current life, there is a certain ease around alcohol, which, hopefully children pick up on and it will help them keep some perspective when they enter the drinking age. Equally, in some households, there are such extreme strictures on drinking—no one is to drink even a drop on any occasion, within the house or outside—this too sometimes works to keep kids off the stuff forever, in a fear-inducing sort of a way.

However, youngsters from either of these ends of the spectrum can get drawn into an unhealthy relationship with alcohol, especially given genetic or other social and emotional factors.

There are some broad dos and don'ts that should be followed in households and families where there is a prevalence of social drinking.

Some families prefer to pull out the drinks once the kids have been fed and put to bed or at least have gone to their room to play with the other kids, etc. But nowadays, rare is the home where kids sleep well before the parents—there seems to be little or no separation between 'adult' and 'children' time and space. If you like to drink, it may be a good idea to bring that separation back as far as is naturally possible.

One thing that should be strictly watched and completely discouraged is adults asking youngsters to fetch and carry the alcohol, the soft drinks, ice, and other paraphernalia. Children should not be co-opted into the process in this way, even if they are not actually drinking.

Alcohol should be kept away, not necessarily under lock and key, but in its own place—what I mean is, not casually here and there. This helps to send the message out to kids that drinking in the family is an adult and responsibly indulged-in activity.

Do make it a point to have fun with the children when there is no drinking involved. Perhaps at a picnic or a lunch, or a brunch with your adult friends and your kids. This way, kids don't associate all manner of enjoyment with the presence of alcohol. Or to put it the other way round, this prevents children from growing up to believe that there's no real partying without alcohol.

Dos and Don'ts

- ઙ Whether there is little or no drinking in the family, the most important thing is to keep one's attitude to alcohol real.
- ઙ As far as possible, drinking should be projected to kids as something enjoyable and yet not absolutely essential to enjoyment and celebration of any kind.

B for

❧

Bigotry

Children tend to pick up offensive and prejudiced ideas about other communities or certain classes of society. Educate and expose your children in a way that liberates them from stereotypes.

Isha's eleven-year-old daughter Mia picks up all kinds of prejudices and biases from her peers. A few weeks ago she came home and made some anti-Muslim statements that horrified everyone. Her parents sat her down and tried to logically argue out these prejudices but she kept saying 'Vinita (a girl in her class) is always right, Vinita is telling the truth.' Then came 'Hitler was a great man.' Recently, she made racist comments about Africans, and this time her source was someone else. Isha and her husband are very keen to teach Mia to think these things out for herself and not be swayed by every little prejudicial propaganda statement that she hears.

Yes, it is chilling when your child comes home with regressive ideas and statements. They are experiencing first-hand themselves, while intolerance and baseless prejudice is all around us. How not to let this affect our and our children's lives is a key issue. Just as the TB germs, which are everywhere, and to fight it we have to build our immunity and resistance, your child too is going to hear half-baked theories, bigoted ideas, and downright ugly talk as she grows up, and will parrot them. How do you give her enough internal resources that prevents her from 'buying into' all this?

First, like with all prejudices—against the poor, other communities, nations, colour—'knowing better' is the first counter-strategy. So instead of putting out blanket and abstract statements like 'Hitler was bad' or 'Africans are wonderful people', or 'don't speak ill of Muslims', try exposing your child to actual people of other communities and economic groups and nationalities if possible; talk about other countries, their history—of course in age-appropriate doses. But don't overwhelm her with information! What I'm saying is, put a face to all these 'themes' in the 'us and them' construct on which prejudice thrives.

It's really interesting and heartening too, the way prejudice rapidly vanishes with exposure to those very cultures and ways of life that people were wary or critical of without knowing them first-hand. Once a person gets to know people from a particular community, race, or sub-group they have been prejudiced about in the past, they find themselves feeling foolish at the sweeping generalizations that they have made all these years. It's that much easier to modify bigotry with children who are more open to new experiences and inputs. Tolerance, then, comes more naturally, when kids learn to recognise and respect different choices—of worship, food habits, dress, and customs. That is a more genuine and practical tolerance, rather than the one that comes from banning politically-incorrect statements and forcing people to say good things about each other without knowing one another.

The second 'strategy' with children like Mia is to subtly bring out the fact that the kids who are feeding her this stuff are ignorant and are parroting other ignorant people. Once you have inserted the idea that blanket statements of hate/intolerance come from small and underexposed minds, you have got your foot in the door!

Thirdly, one must get schools to tackle this issue, again not in a fake 'one-nation–one-world' kind of rah-rah mode, but in a more nuanced and dimensional way. This will go a long way in moulding impressionable minds on this subject. Perhaps you and other like-minded parents could offer to teach such a module regularly with different age-groups. It would need to be conducted with the aim of providing exposure rather than just lecturing, because kids, and adults, don't take well to lectures.

Lastly, I would also advise you to not over-react to these early statements since young kids should be allowed to go through their current experiences on their own, with you providing a broader canvas and perspective in the background. Have faith that the way you as a family live and interact with other people, your attitudes and your world-view, your beliefs in what is right and good, will percolate to your kids.

Dos and Don'ts

- Try exposing your child to people of other communities and economic groups and nationalities if possible. Tolerance and acceptance will come. Celebrating different festivals with people of a particular community is another wonderful way.
- Subtly point out to your child how people who carry these prejudices and biases are small-minded and ignorant.
- Get schools to tackle this issue, not in a preachy way but in a more nuanced and dimensional manner.

Bribery

As adults, we recognize the difference between a reward and a bribe. It is the same ethic that needs to be applied while dealing with children. Encourage them with rewards and treats when they do well. But bribes are a complete no-no.

Anchal is a young mother of a four-year-old, and has been very cautious not to bribe her son when she wants him to do something that he is reluctant to do. However, she sees parents around her calling their bribes 'incentives', and she would like to know how to make a distinction. She feels that it is a bribe when parents can't get their kids to do anything without incentives.

There's a very thin line between what constitutes a bribe and an incentive. But if we borrow from the adult world, perhaps we can use the same logic to make a distinction. Say, I work in an organization that builds roads and my organization offers me an incentive—for every project completed well and on time, I get some extra payment, a bonus, and a letter of commendation—this is an incentive for me to work well on future projects. In addition, if the company sends me a nice box of chocolates upon completion, or takes all the hard-working employees out for a great meal, then that is a reward. However, if, to do that same work I ask my client or my senior officer (who is part of a chain) for money, and I am paid it, then that is a bribe. Moreover, I make it clear that nothing moves ahead unless I get that money, then it means that I just can't or won't function unless I am paid that amount. This means that I have no interest or integrity when it comes to doing the job itself. Building a road means nothing to me, unless my palms are greased.

Isn't it quite the same when parents, desperate to have their children study/eat/play/sleep/behave, get held to ransom by their kids, and accept the fact that nothing will move unless a 'bribe' is paid? That's very different from the parent who expects that something will be done by their child, but 'sweetens the deal' by throwing in a promise of a meal out or a vacation or even a simple toy or favourite sweet or shiny paper star on the softboard. It's also different from the parent who, on seeing that the child has done something well, rewards him or her with something. These two parents' actions are very different from those of the parent who ends up bribing a child to do something.

The essential difference is that the children in the incentive and reward scenario accept that something needs to be done—homework or tidying up or bathing or brushing their teeth just like the road-department person who accepts that this is his or her work. However, the child in the bribing scenario has, like the corrupt road-maker, decided (and been

24

allowed to) that they don't need to or want to do anything. Someone has to 'make' them do it: By bribery or later by threats and dire punishments.

In essence: children of parents, who bribe, are children who have never been taught the intrinsic value of doing something. Children of parents, who give incentives and rewards, have learnt that a thing needs to be done, and while it may not always be fun, that is the only way out. And for that understanding and the fact that he or she does the job, his parents are happy to give him something.

Dos and Don'ts

- ✒ A reward or incentive to a child is to 'sweeten the deal' at the end of a job well done. It is a bonus for a duty that was anyway meant to be done.
- ✒ Do not 'bribe' the child for something you want him/her to do. This will create a situation where the child will have no motivation to perform unless he is always promised something in return.

Bullies

❧

Bullies are often a part of your child's growing up years. If you feel things are getting increasingly difficult for your kid on account of the school or neighbourhood bully, do not hesitate to confront the other child firmly, but with tact.

Six-year-old Raghav's parents moved to a new society a year ago. The boy quickly made friends in the building and enjoyed playing there, until ten days ago. Now none of the children talk to him saying that ten-year-old Manish (who is somewhat a 'leader' of all the younger kids) has told them not to. After four days of no one talking to him, Raghav's mother approached their neighbour's seven-year-old who also said that he can't talk to her son unless Manish 'gives permission'. Raghav is devastated and even though his mother has tried to take him swimming and do other stuff three evenings a week, he needs and wants his peers as company instead of his mom. He has begun to show signs of utter dejection, and asks his mom, 'Why does everyone hate me?'

In the situation, the best one can do is talk to the bullying kid or his parents directly. If you have the nerves, and think you can swing it, you could first, in front of all the kids (without your son present), just in passing stop by the bully and ask him nicely but in a firm, adult-to-adult way, whether he has asked the other kids to shun your son. If he denies it, then he looks less like a leader in front of the other boys, and you can swiftly and smoothly say, 'oh, okay, everyone seems to have misunderstood', and soon get your son down to play. And then watch how it goes. Hopefully things will get back to normal. If this continues, however, or if the bully openly says that he has indeed asked the other kids not to speak to your son then you're up against a real problem child.

In such a case, go to the bullying child's home, and try to speak to his parents, stating that your son is younger, and new in the block and needs a little sensitivity. Hopefully his parents will show some understanding and be able to get their son to behave. Bullies are a bore, and not brave or bold, is the message you will have to subtly send out—not just to your son, but to the other kids too.

Dos and Don'ts

- Confront the bully directly and ask him what the problem is.
- If that doesn't work, speak to his parents.
- Reiterate how bullies are just scared people from inside.

C for

Camp

❧

Quite a few parents tend to feel nervous about summer camps because they think it takes their children away from the protected environs of their homes. This is a mental block that parents need to slowly get past.

During Diwali or summer vacations, there are lots of advertisements for residential camps. Meera has a five-year-old son who is quite out-going, but despite her relatives and friends advising her to send him for one of these camps, she hasn't gathered the courage to do so. She feels that she will not be depriving him of anything really.

While she may not be depriving him of the experience of summer camp, it can be a worthwhile experience for children. It is good for kids to have varied experiences at the right stages of their lives, and this is not something that only the mother can or should provide. The mother could examine why she is so hesitant to send him. Is it anxiety about his safety? If it is, then you should see for yourself if the camp you are sending the child to is safe, with caring adults constantly watching over your kids. Once you have decided to send your child, choose a summer camp carefully; do an extensive research on the various camps. Find parents who have sent their kids before and ask them about the kind of arrangements that were there. Talk to the organizers, get a feel of what kind of people they are. Once you're comfortable with what you see and hear, you'll find it easier to consider sending him.

If your child seems to be prepared to go out and explore, I would advise you to let him go. Initially, he could go just for a day-camp and gradually allow him to go to one that involves spending the night away from you.

Or are you experiencing a deep sense of unease about your son being out of sight and out of your ambit, doing his 'own thing' without you?

Why don't you also do dry-runs, which could start with, if possible, sending him for a few hours to a friend's place, or to sleep overnight at a friend or relative's place? This way, both of you will have a sense of what it feels like, and yet it will not be as big a step such as going off to camp. For starters, you could also just have him go off somewhere for a few hours at a stretch (including a meal time) with his father, without you micro-managing or remote-controlling the outing.

Your anxiety and unwillingness are understandable, it's something all mothers of young children experience. But let this be a 'practise' time for you as well as your son, to prepare for a healthy, untroubled approach to the process of his forming a sense of self, separate and distinct from his mother. Equally important, he (and you) must slowly get used to the idea that there is a whole world to be discovered out there, and it can't be done only via mummy. This is a crucial aspect of growing up—for both mother and the child.

Dos and Don'ts

- Do not be over-protective when your child wishes to be a part of a summer camp or any such outdoor activity. Make adequate enquiries and ensure safety.
- If you are still unsure about it, begin slowly, by allowing your child to spend a night at a friend's or relative's place.

Career Counselling

Many children have no idea what a career entails even if they talk in terms of becoming an engineer, scientist or pilot. If the career counselling sessions offered in your child's school are of little help, get innovative. Organise a group activity where children can talk to people from various fields who are happily pursuing their chosen vocations.

Schools have career counselling for kids from the 9th and 10th class. However, Radha and Atul and other parents that they know feel that neither do the kids seem to get anything from this, nor do the parents feel helped. Mostly the advice is typically hierarchical: Doctor, engineer, software developer up there on top, and then all the 'others' depending on how you have been faring at school. Radha and Atul and a few other parents feel that their kids need career guidance from the 7th standard onwards to get an idea of their own strong and weak points, and also about the many interesting careers that are out there. Is it too early to talk to them about work-life balance, etc?

A group of about ten parents can do this, without

involving formal career counselling institutes or counsellors. Career counselling is an on-going process, and not just a one-shot exercise. Your kids are still young enough not to have to make hard and fast choices (as older ones have to after Board exams). It's best to, at this stage, expose them to, and nurture different skills and likings, and let kids know that some of these can turn into careers, some can be serious hobby-pursuits, or a person can even look at a two-career life, etc.

Since there are a few other parents involved, who feel the same way as Radha and Atul, here's what they could do. Between them all, come up with a small list of the various people that they know who are deeply and happily into their own careers - mainstream as well as unusual ones. Arrange for a day-spend for the kids, or a few hours in an office or in the field with these people, if they are willing. Do this as a once or twice a month activity, on-going. Make it clear to the children that they don't have to choose and decide anything right now. Make it clear to the people who they meet, too, that they have to only expose the kids to their work-day, and not heavily guide or influence them.

The most important thing that comes out of such an exercise is that kids as well as parents stop focusing on the so-called 'solid' 'traditional' careers, and interact with self-actualized people from so many different fields. This exercise means that they also meet people from the mainstream careers who approach their working life with enthusiasm and not just as a road to 'money success' and 'stability' and all those words that mean little to youngsters. So many youngsters don't actually have any real idea what an engineer or an architect or a doctor does in the day. Part of on-going career counselling would be for your kids to get a good sense of a working day or a working week of some of these careers.

As for work-life balance, it may seem like too abstract and adult a concept right now, but you can find ways to relate it to the balance kids themselves have to maintain between school work and play. More importantly, if you yourself as a parent as well as other adults around the child do actually walk-the-walk on work-life balance, and not simply talk-the-talk, that itself goes a long way in teaching kids to give appropriate time to work and to play.

Dos and Don'ts

- Career counselling is an on-going thing, and not just a one-shot exercise. There is no hurry to make the child decide what he wants to do right in adolescence or early teens.

- Expose them to various fields, nurture his different skills and likings, and allow them to think beyond 'conventional' careers.

Conservation

Only a handful of urban households are conscientious about not wasting water and electricity. Which means, most children are not bothered about issues such as conservation, and neither are these values adequately inculcated in them by parents.

Eleven-year-old Anand learns about conservation in school, yet at home he rarely puts any of those principles in practice. He might score top marks in the subject but at home, he's happy to let the water run while he brushes his teeth in the morning or leave the lights or the television on when he walks out of a room. His mother nags him constantly about these things but, unfortunately, his father, and now even Anand, laugh at her, mocking her for being a tree-hugger. We need to stop just talking about conservation with our kids and start teaching them to practice it instead. Firstly, for your family to know that this is not some fad, but a real and tangible conservation strategy, that you're pushing onto your kids you could tell them about initiatives such as the 'Stop Leaking Taps' drive in Mumbai. They had estimated that 6 million litres of water are wasted every day because of leaking taps!

Given the global water crisis looking over us, it really is time that we have our kids connect, really connect, to the issue of using water carefully and thoughtfully. It's ironic that even after Environment Studies being introduced as a 'subject' in school, most urban kids, many parents and even teachers don't apply its lessons in their day to day lives. Of course they will go about making projects and presentations in school on Water and Drought and The Farmer but at home they brush their teeth for ten sleepy minutes, the water running abundantly out of the taps while they attend to their pearly whites. They will drink half a glass of water and toss the rest into the sink. They simply won't notice that in their very own homes, expensive, treated water trickles quietly away from leaking taps, overflowing toilet flush tanks, while they parrot platitudes taught in school about the earth and its resources. They too are learning the art of tokenism, the mouthing of the right things at the right place; and they are learning young.

Ever so often, we are staring into the hard dry eyes of a drought. But what is our (us, urban Indian types) response? We continue hosing down our cars with water, then with soap water, then wash it with some more water. We water our gardens, we wash our balconies and patios every morning. We have two baths a day, we wash clothes that we've worn for an hour, we install fountains, we let water run and overflow in buckets while we chat on the phone—enough of it to water two non-urban households. We throw away 'stale' drinking water, and fill up some 'fresh' water. On top of it we use that well-worn conversation piece: "I tell you, future wars are not going to be about territory, religion or oil . . . they're going to be Water Wars."

We were not like this. Generations of Indians have grown up doing their homework on the reverse of paper that has been on one side. Householders routinely made a neat pile of pink and yellow newspaper bills, flyers, notices, etc, clipped it to an exam board, and used the reverse for lists, notes, messages. Vegetables were bought in your own bag and sorted at home, instead of in ten wafer-thin plastic bags. Shower baths were considered plain silly, and a steaming bucket of water was enough for even the most fanatically clean to have a satisfying bath. Children were clipped on the head for spilling or wasting water, and the only time that they really indulged their inclination to play with water was in rivers or streams and during the rains—not in screaming water parks.

Dos and Don'ts

- One way you could shock your family into getting your point, is for one whole day, putting aside in a large bin or tub or in buckets, measure for measure, all the extra water that you think they are letting go down the drain with their habits.

- While our planners talk of cloud seeding, water harvesting and conservation, we should keep working at getting the family to master that one small gesture: turning off the tap.

Coping

ॐ

Families having children with special needs, medical advice and face-to-face counselling can greatly help the parents as well as the afflicted child and his or her siblings.

Aarav was operated on at the time of his birth for 'hirschsprung disease'. Due to the disease, a part of his colon was without sensation, and he was not able to pass his motions at that time. A timely operation cured him of the problem, however the parents had to take extra efforts to toilet train him. Now he is 8 years of age. However he still has the habit of passing his motions early morning while asleep, in bed. The parents have tried various means of explaining to him or with fear tactics, to stop this habit, but he is unable to stop the same. Though he understands that what he is doing is wrong, he finds himself helpless.

Whether Aarav is completely and genuinely unable to control his bowels, or whether it is now only a delayed toilet training issue, is a difficult call for parents in this situation to take. For all parents dealing with children with congenital conditions and disorders of this kind, there is a need to constantly weigh between making allowances for the child's condition, and insisting on behavioural protocols in line with all other 'normal' children. Many parents in this situation talk about how exhausting and demanding this aspect of the situation is. Both the child and its parents have since birth have to deal with doctors, hospitals, medication, surgical procedures, critical care and after-care, difficult decisions, financial issues. There are many social repercussions of the child's condition. In this case, that an 8-year-old is not able to indicate that he needs to move his bowels, also becomes a socially awkward situation when it comes to going on vacation, staying in other people's homes, having house guests, etc. Toilet training can in itself be a frustrating part of parenting—and more so with your son's particular situation.

All of this takes its own toll of the family's psychological well-being, and stress is bound to build up in both, the parents as well as the child (and any other children, grandparents, etc in the family). Such families must seek out counselling as well as support groups, either in their own town/city or on the Internet.

Dos and Don'ts

- A good family doctor as well as your child's specialist-consultant may be the best people to help you find other parents in the same or similar situations. Talking to them is likely to help you come up with coping strategies and concrete solutions.

- Equally, parents of kids with conditions that need close monitoring and handling, need to focus on their own physical health, as the demand on their mind, body and energies is even more than on other parents.

D for

Death

Death in the family will confuse and unsettle your child. Allow him/her to go through the process of experiencing loss as well as experiencing rejuvenation in some form. Let the 'life moves on' theory slowly work its way.

Maureen's six-year-old daughter had been very close to her grandmother, who passed away. Her grandmother had been unwell, but had led a full, happy life. However, the child is unable to reconcile herself to the death and is gripped with fear that her parents will suddenly die too. When the child had to be rushed to hospital after a sudden asthma attack, she was trembling in fear and confided in her mother later that she thought she too was going to die. How does one explain the idea of death, its inevitability as also something not necessarily immediate, to such a young child?

The child is going through a phase where she has encountered death at close quarters for the first time. At such a time, just about everything happening around her will be 'pinned' to that event for a while. It's like there is suddenly a new lens through which life has to be viewed—

the phenomenon of death and dying. No doubt this is a traumatic time for children, but be assured that children will process the startling and horribly final parting from her grandmother in ways that distress you, but are appropriate for her. As a parent your or her parents' job is to gently 'un-pin' that event from the current life. So that she does not think of death as something lying in wait right round the corner. How do you do that?

First, by letting her grieve fully about the grandmother and yet have a sense of continuity—perhaps put up a picture, add a small ritual (like doing namaste to the photograph every morning), perhaps the mother can wear some small piece of jewellery the grandmother used, or cook her favourite dish once in a while, etc. In this way, the distressing absence is softened, and yet the fact of her demise is firmly and gently re-inforced. Such rituals can replace some of the traditional ceremonies that help people deal with death.

A second 'un-pinning' step would be to involve the child, subtly, in life-cycle-avowing activities like nurturing a plant, a pet, going on nature walks, meeting other old people with whom she can relate to, etc. Most adults are at least somewhat prepared for death - what it is to lose someone we know. We also know what it is to 'move on' because we have experienced it. The child needs to go through the process of experiencing loss as well as experiencing rejuvenation in some form—this is where you can help her along.

Coming to terms with death can be a lifelong process, but it does not have to be a traumatic one. Before embarking on an explanation or a reassuring talk with our children about death, we need to examine our own feelings and beliefs so that we can talk to them as naturally and soothingly as possible.

Where we have doubts, an honest 'I just don't know the answer...I wonder too', may be a more comforting response than an explanation which we don't really believe ourselves.

Dos and Don'ts

❧ Young children expect parents to be all-knowing—even about death. While not all our answers may be completely comforting, we can share what we truly believe. Where we have doubts, an honest, 'I just don't know the answer...I wonder too,' is good enough.

Depression

Marital discord between parents is a big reason for children slipping into depression. A stressful atmosphere at home is sure to cause problems in children. Also remember that their signs of depression are not quite the same as those seen in adults.

With news reports about really small children, some as young as nine and ten years old, attempting suicide, many parents are very worried about what is going on in their kids' minds and whether they too will toy with drastic measures if unhappy about something. It's essential that we prevent kids from going into depression about minor matters as also with the bigger challenges of life.

While some of these cases possibly come from genetic factors and/or families and situations where there are extreme but hidden reasons such as an abusive or dysfunctional parent, or a family tragedy for such young children to go into deep depression, yes the concern is understandable. Firstly, how do we know when a child is depressed or heading towards depression? We are not talking about momentary sadness or being out-of-sorts, but clinical depression. Firstly, depressed kids do not look like depressed adults—rather than being sad and withdrawn, they are often irritable. In fact, at times it can easily be confused with attention deficit hyperactivity disorder. Some depressed kids are also prone to displaying elated moods, grandiose thoughts and daredevil acts, which can look very much like hyperactivity.

There are of course genetic factors at play too, and all depressed children don't necessarily come from dysfunctional homes, but what are the factors that are reasonably in the hands of family members to ensure a positive home atmosphere?

Festering and ugly family relationships should not be discussed and acted upon in front of kids.

Money worries and strategies need not be discussed and agonized over around children. Giving a realistic idea of disposable income and liabilities to older kids is a good idea, but constant money talk—earning it, spending it, comparing other families' living standards, etc.—is something that begins to weigh down on even very young children. Marital discord, even overt, is of another important hidden factor that many children react to with depression. It is absolutely essential that both parents be reasonably contended with themselves and with each other. Many families pour love and affection on their children, but the atmosphere between the two parents may sometimes be joyless or even hostile. This simply has to be worked on, if kids are to feel genuinely supported and secure in the family.

Talk of hopelessness, public apathy, corruption, scams, murders, 'how the good and hard-working get nowhere and the crooks always win', have become the subject matter of dinner-time conversation nowadays. Surely there are many better more positive things in the world to talk about with our kids.

Regular food and sleeping habits as well as adequate light, fresh air, and exercise are other factors that steadies down a child—these are obvious and much-talked about lifestyle issues, but not followed a whole lot in many families.

Family setbacks, whether it is bad grades that a child brings home, or something like a parent losing a job or money, or illness, should be seen and projected to kids as isolated incidents that need remedying, and not as a sign of having continuous bad luck, or as divine punishment, and other such overwhelming interpretations.

Teaching and encouraging our kids to freely participate in loving acts, as well as to receive love with grace and gratitude, on a daily basis and not only on birthdays and festivals, is another key to stability and a feeling of security for our kids; it is also some kind of an insurance against feelings of isolation and alienation.

Dos and Don'ts

- Couples should do their best to avoid fighting in the presence of children.
- Do not create a crisis situation when there is a family set-back. Treat it as a temporary, solvable problem.
- Keep the conversation at home pleasant and do not sort out couple or family issues that may get heated and nasty in front of the kids.

Detached Attachment

There is simply no reason to feel guilty that you have a life beyond your kids and that you do not feel the need to constantly hover around the children or micro-manage their lives.

Meenakshi has two children, aged thirteen and eleven. She loves her kids, but is beginning to wonder if she is less of a parent because she is not 'into' them the way a lot of her friends are. They are not on her mind all the time, and she finds herself seeking out adult company over being with them for at least two days of the week. She sees how other parents meet up with their friends or relatives only if it involves the kids, or if the kids are occupied in school or something else. She worries that she may come across as a cold mother to her kids, because they must notice how much attention other parents give to their kids. Meenakshi has thought about this, and she is not cold towards them at all. It's just that, in all honesty, they are not the centre of her universe. She also doesn't understand why many of her friends are constantly worried about their kids. She never worries about them and their future. Similarly, her husband Vikas has no self-doubt on this front.

There are as many parenting styles as there are fingerprints. Today, we see a large number of urban parents who are completely focused on their kids. However, that does not make parents like Meenakshi 'neglectful' or 'derelict in their duty' as parents. In fact, parents with friends and pursuits of their own outside their parenting activities are likely to be less stressed and give their kids less stress too!

There is much debate about 'helicopter' versus 'hands-off' parenting. While the constantly hovering parent (the helicopter) may be appearing to be a more committed one, rest assured that this is not what kids need or really benefit from. Creativity, lateral thinking, a better developed sense of self, learning from mistakes, and learning how to entertain oneself are some of the downstream advantages for a child who is not constantly watched, regulated, and taught what to say, think, and do.

As for the issue of 'appearing cold' to the kids, genuine love and caring, even if not demonstrated all the time, is what come through to our kids clearly. I would urge parents not to be defensive and troubled about this, if you are indeed not a neglectful parent in the real sense of the word. Being 'worried' for our kids is the neurotic and anxious form of what should be 'concern' for our kids. Free-floating worry— about the future, about grades, about health—will only create an atmosphere of aggravation rather than demonstrate a parent's love for their child. Many grown people in my counselling sessions complain about how they carried around the burden of guilt over their parents' 'sacrifices' and about how much their parents worried for them. This is surely not a recipe for a happy childhood. I would urge parents to gain the same kind of self-confidence, like Meenakshi's husband, about the way you relate to your kids. This kind of detached attachment is a more balanced way of being with your children, particularly as they grow into mature youngsters.

Do and Don'ts

- Do not feel guilty about adopting a relaxed-loving attitude towards your kids.
- Don't feel the need to explain yourself vis-à-vis other parents who may choose to not have much of a life outside their parenting duties.

Disciplinary Options

There is no question that discipline is an inherent part of child raising. The question is how do you approach this unpleasant task as a parent and make it constructive and the lessons long-lasting?

One hears how corporal punishment and strong, sarcastic words as well as social humiliation are not just wrong but they are of no use in getting children to follow rules or work hard. All counsellors (and all parents and teachers when they are calm) agree with this. But those who work closely with kids, like Mr Sohum, the principal of a residential school, and parents too, are often besieged with the question: how does one get the job done, when a child just does not follow rules, or is disruptive to the other kids and their learning? Surely there have to be consequences for bad behaviour?

Yes, there have to be consequences, and learning lessons about the consequences of our behaviour is an extremely important part of the maturing process. Many maladjusted and dysfunctional people are those who have no sense of the consequences of their actions and decisions.

In teaching a kid the importance of consequences, to take responsibility for what they do or say, what is needed is disciplinary action not punishment. There is a difference between the two. Random angry punishments are a) handed out from an angry frustrated adult; b) can be harsh and degrading; c) end up making the child think more of the punishment and less of what he/she did wrong.

On the other hand, disciplinary action is something you have a) thought of in advance and planned; b) is never humiliating to a child; c) results in the child being able to think of what he did wrong and make amends in a reasonable way.

I would divide disciplinary action into two categories:

1) **Time-out**: in which some privileges are taken away and the child has to do something constructive during this time out;
2) **Giving back what you took away**: Making good whatever loss he has caused to someone or something.

Examples from both categories need to be thought out and planned creatively, so that you can choose one of them and use them appropriately depending on what the child has done wrong.

Time out could be withdrawing of TV or gaming time or some other privilege. However, don't leave the child to just simmer around the house or outside the classroom, couple it with an hour of silence, or getting him to read something out loud, or if it is in a school setting, then make him/her go to the library and write down something to do with the subject that was being taught when he was being disruptive.

'Giving back' can be in the form of some physical task (see, it is physical, but not at all humiliating) that needs to be done in the house or school, like cleaning up, carrying, planting, digging, or kitchen-duty. Some other examples are going to a younger class and reading something to the kids, or helping to fill registers in the school's admin office. You could also fine a child by making her give up something of her own and give it away. Come up with things that are demanding and engrossing to do, but not so much fun for them. Avoid tasks that are impossible or monotonous ('I will be tidy' written 100 times is a non-option!).

The great thing about these kinds of reprimands is that the child is likely to come out feeling chastised but not traumatized. Also, adults who mete out these disciplinary actions do not feel terrible later, as they usually do when they slap/isolate/tongue-lash a child.

Dos and Don'ts

- Disciplinary action should not be punishments handed out by an angry parent.
- Do not humiliate your child under the name of disciplining.
- Come up with creative and well-thought out ideas to make your child realize the consequence of his/her actions.

Discord

Children are deeply affected when they see disharmony at home. To see parents involved in bitter fights causes severe depression among them.

Shalini and her husband have what can only be called a 'working marriage'. Basically, they are keeping the unit together for their children. There is not much affection, but there are no open fights either. Whatever problems they have, the couple deal with it in private. Shalini tells her son, aged thirteen, to concentrate on studies and not give importance to anything else happening around. However, his grades are slipping and he is quite withdrawn. How can she insulate him from her marital situation?

Parents going through marital discord need to concentrate on their child's emotional well-being instead of focusing all energies on that dubious one-point programme of 'academic excellence'. Remaining in a marriage for the sake of the children is a thing that a lot of people do, but that is simply not enough anymore. So if you do know that you are going to remain in the marriage 'for the children', you will have to come up with a way of dealing with each other and family issues that ensures a degree of dignity, mutual respect and affection, if not love. This is the minimum a child needs to see between his parents, or else it is a bit of a sham to think that merely remaining under the same roof ensures stability to the children.

'He's fast asleep', 'she's too small to understand', 'he didn't hear anything'—how often do we as adults convince ourselves that our children are not in any way affected by adult fights/arguments/unpleasantness? In fact, we tell ourselves that if an incident of this kind did not take place right in front of a child, then he hasn't even registered it, so where's the question of being affected by it. It is time we fully recognized that our children are deeply affected by even the unsaid and unexpressed in the household.

Of course, every family has its ups and downs, rifts, reconciliations, and arguments, but what is pivotal is how these are handled, and how they come across to your kids. If adult relationships around a child are basically good, strong, respectful and trusting, then a child is able to take a certain degree of disagreement, raised voices, or unhappy silences in her stride. It is when fights in the household signal that there is an absence of love, mutual trust, and respect between the adults, that a child begins to be badly affected.

Children today are brought to doctors and counsellors for depression, lack of concentration, slow physical growth, eating disorders. Most people tend to lay the blame on 'external distractions' such as TV, video games, fast food, and others. However, in at least seven out of ten cases, there is a fairly serious relationship problem that the child is 'witness' to in his household. Again, there may be nothing openly wrong, but there are often undercurrents of discord that play a key role in unsettling a child and make him or her vulnerable to all kinds of disorders, emotional and physical. The adults in a house may individually shower a child with attention, facilities, love, praise and yet, if the interpersonal relationships between these adults are unpleasant, even covertly so, much of what is showered on the child simply slides away, not nourishing him at all.

Dos and Don'ts

- Children thrive on harmony and hope, and if these are absent in their homes, their spirit shrivels.
- No amount of 'pretend happiness' between adults can fool a child. We simply have to provide them the real thing by working genuinely on our own relationships.

Divorce

Be upfront with your teenage children if your marriage is not working, but jointly create a cover of parental love, support, and security so that they know that their lives won't be dramatically altered.

Abha and Bipin, parents of two teenagers, are about to get divorced. Since the kids are at a boarding school, the mother and father believe that the children are unaware of the problems between them. They are now wondering how to break the news of the divorce to the kids.

All children in such situations deserve to be told the facts as they are, in straight, simple, and truthful terms. When children have no idea about any marital strife between their parents, they are bound to be shocked if they are told about it out of the blue and will ask what the problem is. Parents in such a situation need to be prepared with a mutually agreed-upon reply. Their versions must match, as it is very distressing for kids if parents begin to argue about why they are divorcing right in front of them, while they are trying to break it to them. If parents find it hard to arrive at a common 'version' of why they are divorcing, it would make imminent sense to take the help of a counsellor or well-wisher. At all costs, avoid the risk of giving children conflicting messages about a divorce and its possible impact on them.

Children or teenagers faced with this situation sometimes try to get into the nitty-gritty of their parents' marital problems, hoping desperately to sort it out for them. Discourage this gently, telling them that events have gone beyond that. Underline the fact that the parents are parting on decent and amicable terms.

Telling them is one step; keeping the lines of communication open for the weeks following this revelation is the other important move. While you as an adult can look ahead and see how the new arrangements and alignments can be worked with minimum damage, your children cannot see it that way right now.

Assure them that you have decided to part ways, but that you remain their parents in all sense of the term. Many children as well as teenagers fear in a divorce situation that they will lose one of their parents, or worse, be forced to divide their loyalties and 'choose' whose 'side' they are on. You must clearly articulate that you respect each other as parents, and do not want anyone to be on anyone's side. Do not use the children to inflict collateral damage. You will, therefore, be able to assure your kids that though your marriage may be ending, you can cooperate as their parents, always. For all of this to happen, parents need to avoid the adversarial stances that lawyers and misguided advisors may instigate you to take.

Some children feel anxious that a divorce means that they will now be abandoned in some way, and that they will have to fend for themselves. Both parents need to convey through their words and deeds that they will always be there for them. Let them know that you have a gameplan. It may not, of course, sound to them as good as when you were together as a family, but at least they will be assured that their parents are accounting for them in all future plans.

Some kids are known to 'introject' the whole situation, not showing much on the surface, but assuming that somehow they may have 'caused' the split. Children are known to think that if only they had behaved better or done better at school, their parents would have been happier, and therefore remained together. If you get any sense of this, be very clear with your children that your divorce has absolutely nothing to do with them.

Dos and Don'ts

- Give your children time to absorb—there will be tears, or anger, or sometimes no reaction at all. Sensitively let them remain with those emotions, and avoid papering everything over with too many words.
- As for the departing parent, the one who will see less of them, it is critical to remain genuinely connected with the children, so that the sense of loss and unhappiness can be minimized.

E for

Elitism

Putting your child in an elite school might will benefit him/her in terms of better education and facilities, however, there are some challenges…parents need to ensure that their kids don't turn into snobs.

Deepak and his wife Sona are planning to send their six-year-old son to a premium school where the academic and extra-curricular scene is great. However, they fear that an environment of exclusively privileged kids will translate into snobbery, materialism, and an absence of positive exposure to people from other social stratas. Down-to-earth schools are better on these counts, but the education they offer is largely unimaginative. It is a common dilemma while choosing schools.

If you're convinced that this premium school does indeed deliver as good an academic and extra-curricular exposure as it promises, then you've got a good reason to put your child there. However, when it comes to the kind of over-exposure to affluence and privilege that you fear, you need to consistently tackle this at home. As he grows, you would need to have age-appropriate conversations with your son about these matters. For instance, when a child asks you the question: 'Why are people poor?' at no point should you give one often used reply, 'Because they did bad things in their previous life' or 'because they are lazy'. You could say something on the lines of: 'because they are unfortunate, sometimes they don't have education, exposure, and opportunities over many generations. Sometimes they don't have sound health.' Usually parents leave it at that but it is important to 'harvest' a child's in-born empathy and altruism and engage the child in some small solution-oriented suggestion—'Should we give your old clothes to the orphanage this year?' or 'This Diwali should we buy a present/sweets/outing for…'(your maid's child or any such person you identify). With slightly older children, you can perhaps encourage them to teach another child or adult to read and write. You would need to lead by example too; it does not need to be a full-time occupation, but an important, weekly/monthly priority activity that you undertake, so that your child sees that you 'put your money where your mouth is'. Else these conversations end up being only guilt-assuaging and feel-good talks. It sounds as mere tokenism.

Foreseeable problems will crop up on two counts. Firstly, surrounded as he will be by kids who get a lot of the latest goodies, are taken on exotic holidays, and live in plush neighbourhoods, he may constantly want you as a family too to 'measure up' to this, which could be a problem if you are unable/unwilling to do so.

Secondly, even if you do intend to provide all those things

to your child, as you have pointed out, you run the risk of him knowing only privilege and nothing about how most the rest of the world lives. Which is not just an insensitive way of growing up, it also cuts a person off from being able to have a broad world-view or to make friends and work with people across cultures. It is a well-documented fact today that many people at the top got there by rising from the ranks, or by being closely aware of and associated with people from various stratas of life during their formative years. Sometimes success can come out of sheer luck but many people say that they grew up seeing their parents or grandparents functioning in a fair, egalitarian manner, and having cordial and mutually beneficial relationships—working or social—with people from various socio-economic brackets.

So if you do put him in an elite school, the onus is on you and your close family and friends to see to it that your child gets genuine exposure to other social stratas and situations. This would entail more than superficial 'eat up your beans, there are children starving in the slums' kind of conversations thrown in once in a while. It would mean seeing to it that he interacts with less privileged kids and people from different stratas, possibly right there in your neighbourhood. And these interactions do not only mean being in a 'charitable' mode, but in normal, everyday situations. This is the only way you can balance out the exclusive and selective nature of his social experience at school.

Dos and Don'ts

- You could have your kids teach someone to read and write or get him to watch a workman in your home, chat with him, share a meal, know more about his life.

- You could also voice your concerns to the school authorities; they may well have some kind of social outreach programme that is genuine. If they don't already have something in place, perhaps you could spearhead some such activity, which does not only involve charity, but *interaction*.

- There may be other parents with the same concerns who would be happy to join in with you to ensure that their kids grow up with well-rounded and inclusive personalities.

Excessive Social Networking

Some parents love to post pictures of their children on social networking sites like Facebook. This is, of course, a personal choice but when one overdoes it, it can give birth to potential problems, as there is some degree of self-consciousness and narcissism embedded in the process.

Nahar's sister, a mother of two kids, puts photos, quotes from everyday conversations, the newly-made interior of her kids' room, and sometimes even small video clips of her kids on Facebook. Her kids have quite a fan following, and she feels that there is nothing wrong with it. The kids are now three and five and this has been going on since their birth. Nahar cannot actually spell out what is wrong with this, but as their uncle he feels there is some breach of the kids' privacy beyond a point, and also fears that some perverted person may have too much access to their private lives, including the place where they live. Over fifty people respond to her uploads each time, which worries him that this is too much of the public being let into the private life. There are details about where they stay, with their new car in the photos and the number plate is clearly visible. Is he being old-fashioned and paranoid here? The only thing he has been able to control is pictures of himself and them, which he has requested her not put up.

The uncle's fears and discomfort are justified, and there are many people out there with the same kind of doubts about the flaunting of children and what they say, eat, do, where or how they sleep, what they wear, etc., in the public space.

Having said that, many people (both those who post and those who loyally follow such posts) don't see anything wrong in this. However, the ethical question here is whether the lack of privacy on a public platform like Facebook is something that the children themselves would like. They are unaware now, but perhaps they may not like it in retrospect when they are old enough to know that their words and actions and various moments were so much in the public domain.

One writer in the *Wall Street Journal* calls it 'oversharenting'—the tendency of parents to share a lot of information and photos of their kids online.

This exhibition of their endearing moments on a social networking site has repercussions for the parents themselves. Quite a few of them are addicted to the activity, and may end up being a kind of scriptwriter, director, and photographer of family life, with one eye a little too often on the number of 'Likes' and 'Awwws' that come in response to every cute picture or quote from their child's day. When there is an awareness of a growing audience out there for what is everyday, personal, and most often spontaneous kids' behaviour, there is going to be some degree of self-consciousness, and (dare I say) narcissism, embedded in the process.

One's fear about the security aspect is well-founded, given that locations, car numbers, other family members are easily identified in these uploads.

Dos and Don'ts

- With families now separated by time and space, the sharing of beautiful moments in a growing family's life is something that grandparents, aunts, uncles, friends, all yearn for, and some of these media are wonderful ways to share.
- Perhaps more discreet privacy settings, and sharing an album through other media, rather than an easily accessible platform like Facebook, could be a better option.

F for

✧

Food Critic

Mothers tend to feel hurt and upset when children display insensitivity in their comments about 'home' food. Parents should treat this with a mix of amusement and tact.

Geeta's fourteen-year-old daughter recently declared: 'I don't like anything that you cook'. Geeta takes a lot of trouble over the food made in the house, whether by her or the visiting cook. It hurts her deeply and moreover she can't order out all the time just to please her daughter. Her daughter often tells Geeta about how the food in other friends' homes is much better than theirs. She often brings back the school tiffin untouched. Geeta is quite distraught.

One of the perfect weapons in an adolescent's armoury is to hit out at mom's cooking. And it hits most mothers right where it hurts! While all of us want our kids to eat well and enjoy home food, it is not possible to please the fast-expanding mind and palette of a fourteen-year-old at all meals. Yes, one could sit her down and ask her what she would like different in her tiffin, but it's also important not to feel so deeply hurt by her comments on the food made at home. Seeking brownie points—constant and comprehensive approval—from our kids on this count is a bit of a pointless exercise on two counts: firstly, you can't win when they compare your cooking to that made in someone else's home and in fast-food places; rest assured that your youngster will keep changing the position of the goal post, if you try to reach the 'other people's cooking' goal! Secondly, they really need to understand that their homes are not places fine-tuned to fulfil their every whim and demand. Nutritious, tasty food on time and in adequate quantities is what most meals should be about, fun and fast food for some meals.

Mothers in this situation need to give themselves the approbation that they seek from their child—for being a parent who provides food and thought-out meals. Also, take heart in the fact that one fine day in the not-too-distant future the same child will miss your food and remember home meals with extreme fondness and yearning and be waiting to come home for your cooking!

Dos and Don'ts

❧ The next time your child talks about someone else's yummy food, try not to be defensive at all. In fact, you could join her in her admiration for that food, and you could even suggest that she finds out exactly how it is made and that perhaps she could try her hand at making it herself or helping you make it that way. Do this just for fun, and not to 'improve' your cooking skills in her eyes.

- Do not appear hurt, defensive, or lecture your child about what food is made in your home. Going into injured pride mode is pointless too—'I'm sorry that's the best I can do, and what can I do if it doesn't measure up to your standards' kind of sulky responses are not called for.
- Avoid going on the offensive and listing all the sheer hard work that goes into keeping house and generating meals.

Foreign Cultures

There is understandable anxiety among parents who are moving to other countries about child-rearing-related laws. It is important to get acquainted with some of the basic legal issues in these countries related to family life.

Bharti and her husband are going for a three-year stay in a European country. Their children are six and three years old. They are quite worried after reading about the Norway case, where authorities took away the children from Indian parents for reasons that at first did not seem valid to us Indians. This is because they feel that there may be laws and protocols related to children which they may not even be aware of, and they may break them without even knowing it. For example, Bharti, her husband, and the children all sleep in the same room. And she does once in a while threaten to spank her son (it's at the most a light rap on the shoulder). Bharti and her husband are both going to be working, but at different timings in the twenty-four-hour cycle.

For parents in these situations, it is important to know that authorities of other countries are not some other species with wildly different parenting rituals from us! It is just that their systems are seriously codified and also followed to the letter.

All laws and protocols for a country are available online, and it would be a good idea for you to go and look it up.

What young Indian families in different parts of the world experience is that some of the details depend a lot on the country that they are going to. 'North European countries are much stricter in their child legislation than Switzerland or France'" is what one couple experiences. Some countries are more culturally attuned to most ethnicities, especially Indians, as there is a sizable population from the sub-continent there.

One strong suggestion is that you chat with the Indian community there or people at your work about laws involving kids in vehicles (not in front, bucket seats, etc.), kids and access to liquor stocks in the house, kids and access to knives and any other dangerous stuff around the house, kids carrying heavy school bags or lunch boxes, kids being left alone at home. If both the parents are working, kids will have to be in day care or have a nanny after school until the parents finish work. Kids can never be alone without adult supervision until they are teenagers.

About sleeping arrangements, continue what you're doing now, but get a sense of what other families do, and maybe you could use this transition to help your kids sleep in their own room. One Indian parent living in the US and a European country says, 'Personal space is very important to people in the West. Babies start sleeping in their own rooms from a young age and this is the way it is. If you can't do this and have a small apartment, or think it's too early, make sure all sleeping arrangements are comfortable. Each in their own bed with comfortable space.'

Some things come without any laws or rules, but are socially acceptable or unacceptable behaviours in another culture. For instance, kids screaming and running around in a restaurant or other public space is currently not a problem at all for most Indians in India. However, in a Western country you would need to instill a sense of public and private spaces. These things you can pick up on by being observant and not anxious.

It is important for parents of young kids going to countries where they have no natural and automatic support system as you may have back home, to find and establish good support services and counsel for themselves too. Long winters, a fair amount of isolation, the newness of everything, homesickness…all of it can affect you. Have some kind of early-warning system in place for yourself, so that you can recognize signs of stress and/or depression. Find out in advance to whom you could turn for counselling help even if it is online, or just to take a day off from parenting on your own. Use some time of day-care systems, maybe once a week. For instance, one young Indian family in Sweden sends all their three kids on Monday and Thursday to day care so that the mother gets some time to herself (either to catch up on extra office work, or for personal time) on one day and father on one day; Sundays and all other times are family time.

Try to find a balance of holding on to your own values or mores, while not being completely cut off from the ways of your host country that may turn your kids into mal-adjusted oddities. A simple example one parent gives is of eating with hand versus using cutlery. You can easily teach your kids do both, with grace and ease, and to know in what situations to use which skill. This is not about submerging one's identity or about standing stiffly apart either. It's about creating a conducive atmosphere for children who need to move between two different cultural milieus at times, between home and the outside world.

Dos and Don'ts

- Chat with the Indian community there or people at your work space about the laws regarding kids.
- Parents need to find and establish good support services and counsel for themselves too. Get a sense of what other families around them do.

G for

Gender Stereotyping

Parents and onlookers often read too much into the preferences their little kids show in their choice of toys. They fear that boys who play with dolls or kitchen sets will grow up to be 'sissies'. And girls who show less interest in dolls and kitchens but more in marbles or computer games 'are going to be poor home-makers'. These are baseless and limiting fears.

Amrita's son is three and he loves playing with dolls—feeding them, crooning them and mock-cooking for them. Neither her husband nor she have an issue with this. But some friends, who have kids of the same age group, were scandalized when her son began playing with their daughter's toys and told her that she should subtly stop him from doing this. Amrita and her husband think that gender-stereotyping is passé really, but how do they handle the people who think it's weird for a boy to play with dolls?

It may be 'passé' in Amrita's book, but it is obviously not so for a lot of people. Getting people to be more 'politically correct' about gender stereotyping doesn't change deep-rooted underlying misconceptions, anxieties, and prejudices.

Moreover, it isn't really crucial that you reason and debate with people who are stuck in these gender stereotypes. What is important right away is that: a) you are totally comfortable with your child playing at whatever makes him or her happy, occupied and well-rounded; and b) your friends do not carry over their attitude into treating your child like some oddity.

Once you are clear on the first point, you'll find yourself able to be at ease with things, and not feel the need to defend your son or reason with people and change their thinking. You simply live your convictions, walk the walk, and don't get drawn into protracted arguments over whether it's right or not for boys to play with dolls. You will then simply dismiss or smile away the 'objections' and not feel the need to explain or defend your son's actions. However, you will have to bluntly draw the line at people saying things to him directly like: 'Hey, are you a little girl, playing with dolls?' Either right there when they say it, or later, when you get a chance, make it clear that this is an attitude you do not subscribe to, and that the person must simply stop making these jeering remarks.

A three-year-old playing at house-keeping with kitchen toys and with dolls is absolutely fine. It's only your friends' homophobia—that too of a rather uninformed and basic kind—that is reading all kinds of things into your kid's interests. You would be doing a small child a huge disservice if you were to cut him off from the shapes, textures, mechanics as well as imaginative play that goes into so-called girlish toys. Rest assured that only good can come from a male child taking on, even in play, the role of a nurturing parent towards the doll. It isn't just that this will make him a better parent, that's for much later. In the immediate here and now, it makes for more consideratenesses, tenderness, and an engagement with household chores as something fun, rather than 'drudgery to be left to the maid and kitchen help'!

It's ironic that people take these natural, healthy care-giving impulses that boys exhibit and turn them into some kind of joke. There is absolutely no evidence that little boys who are allowed to play with dolls grow up to be 'sissies'. In fact, teasing and preventing them from playing with dolls and 'house-house' blocks them off from natural impulses, and forces them to surface later to act in an exaggeratedly masculine way, and to despise any appearance of 'softness' in other boys. And how this affects their way of dealing with girls and later with women is another story!

The same applies to people slotting little girls into stereotypes by never getting them cars or mechanical, sporty toys to play with. Or laughing at those that do.

A word of caution though, in our reverse anxiety that we don't succumb to typecasting, we really shouldn't make a big deal about 'breaking the stereotype' and insisting on getting our kids to play with gender-defying toys. That wouldn't be natural either.

Dos and Don'ts

- Have the courage of your own convictions and do not get into protracted adult-to-adult arguments either between spouses or between a parent and a grandparent or parent and a friend about whether it is right for boys to play with dolls.
- All the same, do not go to the other extreme and insist on your kids playing with gender-defying toys.

Good Guests

&❧

Kids (and their parents) need some guidance and tips on how to behave when they are guests in someone else's home. This will help them to be good guests at every stage of their lives.

The Roshan family are going with their kids aged six and eight to stay with friends for ten days. This is the first time that the kids are going to be house guests, and both parents are a little anxious about how their kids will behave—about the food, sleeping arrangements, sharing toilets and keeping them clean, about the clutter that they may create. They don't want to cramp their kids' style and make them tense, but yes, it is certainly important for kids to know that there is a way in which one can inhabit in someone else's home and keep the stay pleasant.

Setting a few ground rules without straight-jacketing your kids is a good idea when it comes to visiting people. It is a tricky time—how the family as a whole lives in another person's household for ten days will definitely affect whether everyone concerned has a good time, and everyone comes away happy.

Try to go with the flow of the general house-style of your hosts. For instance, respect when they eat and what they eat; if 8 pm dinner is too early for you, remember you're on holiday, and have to do it only for a few days. If your host family is big on Indian food, and you or your kids are simply dying for a Chinese meal, you can eat that on one of your days out. You'll be surprised how many people feel free to comment on their host's food and lifestyle, 'You mean you guys eat dal-roti EVERYDAY?' or 'Gosh, I can't stand soya, how do you guys stomach it?' Even as a joke, it's a no-no. Remember, to tell your kids about this too. This is also not a time for you to declare your family's eating idiosyncrasies, like, My older boy never TOUCHES pav bhaji.' Unless you have a serious medical reason for avoiding foods, you need to keep any food preferences to yourself, unless you're specifically asked.

Follow your host's lead in matters of tidiness too. If he or she keeps an extremely tidy and neat house, do see that your kids don't leave half-drunk water glasses or damp towels around; use coasters on her furniture; help with tidying up the kitchen, etc.

Do not expect your kids to be entertained throughout your stay. While your host will have arranged some outings and entertainment for you, they have to attend to their own chores too, so do try and find ways to get around the place yourself and don't expect your host to play chauffeur and tour guide at all times. Take your children's books and games along with you.

If there are other kids at your friend's house, encourage

your children to play together, but don't force it all the time. Allow kids to veer off in their own direction and read, and not interact with each other all the time. If there are fights, which make things quite awkward, intervene gently and deflect any face offs.

Tell your kids to treat your host's appliances, computers, even light switches, as well as the host-kids' toys with some tentativeness; tell them to not use them without permission. Every home has its own peculiar problems, and you don't want to cause inconvenience by inadvertently tripping the fridge or shorting the water heater.

If your kids have any specific allergies or strong dislikes, try to carry with you some of their specifc needs. Knocking on a tired host's bedroom door at night and asking for a 'pure cotton bedsheet' because synthetics don't agree with your child, is not a good idea.

See that your kids behave politely with elders in the host family and with the daily help too.

Dos and Don'ts

- Preparing children to be in 'guest mode' is a good idea. This does not mean that they have to be straight-jacketed, but parents can teach them to be sensitive to the rules and rhythms of the host's home.
- After a vacation, bring back the old-fashioned art of sending heart-felt thank you notes or cards (emails, texts, any mode of communication), so that kids learn to voice their appreciation.

Gratitude

❧

Children tend to be oblivious at times about the selfless efforts put in by their parents for them. We can instill a sense of gratitude in children from an early age, without guilt-tripping them.

Dilip's fifteen-year-old son is a very talented, budding star-sportsman. However, Dilip feels that he tends to take for granted the small and big things that the adults around him have done for him over the years. How does Dilip get his son to become more aware of and acknowledge the invisible contribution of his parents and his grandfather, in his successes? They have played chauffeur, dietician, counsellor, masseuse, secretary, and emotional supporters to the boy from the time he has taken up swimming over the last seven years, and Dilip gets the feeling that while he does say 'thanks, ma, thanks, appa', he has learnt to take this kind of support for granted. Recently he has shown irritation and impatience when he has been inconvenienced in any way because of some other domestic troubles. He treats it as if 'the system has let him down' and not as with the understanding of a family-member, that on some days arrangements will falter. This is not something the family likes, but they don't know how to change it without sounding as if they are resenting what they did for him all these years.

The process of rearing a child—any child, but particularly one on whom so much attention and hard work has been lavished—to be appreciative and grateful, begins much before the age of 15. Ideally, the seeds for this must be sown early, and not when we see disturbing signs that our kids are taking us thoroughly for granted!

Teaching a child to be grateful and appreciative of what the adults around him or her do for him doesn't mean that we get our kids to feel 'obliged' and 'beholden' to us at all. It really isn't so much about parents feeling validated and appreciated, it's more about the child becoming a better person, when he learns to value what he gets from the world of loving adults around him. While kids necessarily must feel entitled to your love and nurturing of their talents, there is a time when they must see that the adults in their lives provide this sometimes at the cost of their own opportunities and personal goals. It is part of the maturing and development process for a child to see his parents, grandparents, godparents and other concerned and loving adults as people in their own right who go out of their way to enable the growth of a child.

In our anxiety to have our kids become achievers and successful at academics or sports or music or any other special talent, many of us let some of the other simple lessons fall by the wayside, making our star child to start taking all the little, invisible and mundane things taken care of by parents that go into the making of his career for granted. It's important, if we want our kids to keep it real, that we too keep it real.

As for impatience and dismissive behaviour on the part of the fifteen-year-old about some system not working on one particular day and inconveniencing him, this is just not acceptable behaviour. You will be doing your son or daughter a very big favour if you pull him off the road for a bit, and talk to him about this, reminding him gently that the adults in his life are not his staff! You would do well to introduce even a 10-minute window in his day in which he does something selflessly for his mother or grandfather.

Making a child feel secure and special is one thing, but letting him take it all for granted without any appreciation, is bad for a child's own personality development.

Dos and Don'ts

- ❧ However talented, busy and 'in-demand' your child is, expect him or her to do a little stuff around the house, and take note of the needs of all the people that usually provide the invisible solid support.
- ❧ The child must sometimes be called upon to do things in return, to help out with things that adults need help with (cell phones and computers perhaps!).
- ❧ Some parents can also introduce a tiny before-bed or morning ritual of 'giving thanks' to everyone real and spiritual who makes the child's day possible.

H for

Helpful

A bright child who goes out of his way to help others is extremely heartening to see, and also signifies qualities that will take him far. This is a rarity in times when many parents push kids to be self-serving.

Meenal has an odd complaint. Her fifteen-year-old son Arnav is 'too helpful'. As he is very bright, many of his friends take up a lot of his time asking him to explain to them maths and science difficulties. His parents keep telling him that he should concentrate on his own studies, and tell the kids to ask their teachers to sort out their problems.

From what Meenal describes, her son sounds like a fine young man. If his own marks/grades are good, his helping others is an excellent thing, and not a waste of time. Moreover, explaining to others is a revision and clarification for him too. There is no subject in school for 'kindness and helpfulness' but it appears that her son deserves full marks in this life skill.

In the pre-exam hysteria about topping the class and the cut throat competition that exists between peers, we send out wrong messages to our children to 'put themselves first' and not to 'waste time'. So our kids sitting for the 10th and 12th board exams are supposed to eat, study, sleep, be entertained a bit, and that's it. We tell our kids that because they're sitting for their boards, they are free to be a little 'self-serving entity' and let everyone else go to hell.

Ironically, a few years down the line, we will be encouraging our kids as young adults to join workshops, camps and jobs that teach team-building and co-operation. We will also get them to 'volunteer' and teach street kids and other such community service activities, because it will look good on their resume when they apply for Ivy League colleges. Later, we will talk glibly and blithely about living in abundance.

But it's time we took a less self-seeking and miserly hoarder's view of things when it comes to our children's 'progress'. Perhaps it is time we learnt a few life-lessons from the abundant kindness and ease displayed by youngsters like Meenal's son. Since she says that his grades are good, he is obviously not being foolhardy or being taken for a ride or any such paranoid interpretation by others.

We must have our children's overall development in mind at all times. You can't fit together his psyche in bits and pieces like a jigsaw or some kind of modular structure, as if the kindness and consideration component can be an add-on later after he has done with looking out for himself and himself alone! While we encourage our children to work hard and focus and do well in school, there may be (and should be) ample room for them to take other people along too—to share with friends who need a bit of help, and in this way learning way more about life than what any board exam can possibly teach.

Dos and Don'ts

- ❧ Being selfless and helpful is a precious trait in a child and parents must be proud rather than concerned about this.
- ❧ Some of these intangible traits are not measured and rewarded in school, but should be.

High-handedness

When parents catch their kids being high-handed or rude with domestic staff, they have to make it clear that their behaviour is unacceptable. The best lessons come from how you yourself behave with household employees.

I am a US national, currently living in India for a three-year assignment. Our kids, aged six and ten, go to a good school here - where we are happy with the academic standards as well as the values taught and inculcated. The kids have made many friends, and have settled well and are made to feel welcome in many Indian homes. However, what we are finding difficult is how to talk to and relate to the daily help, the chauffeur, the garbage man, the milk delivery boy, etc. While we tend to acknowledge the presence of 'staff', wish them when they come in, give them instructions and not orders, it is different here. I see my kids picking up the imperious or dismissive tone while talking to our staff too, as do their friends. How do I (and do I at all) communicate to my kids that this is wrong, and yet not get into criticizing the local way of doing things? We have always taught our kids to accept and appreciate the differences in attitudes and views in different parts of the world. But on this count, I just don't know.

Some things may be the local custom or habit or deeply entrenched system, but that doesn't make them right. I can see that you're trying hard not to be judgemental here, so let me say it for you: the behaviour of many Indian adults as well as kids towards their daily help and other workers around them ranges from indifferent to being outrightly rude. Many Western visitors here are struck by how we don't even acknowledge the entry or presence of 'servants' in our homes.

Some Indian families and homes do bring up their children to talk politely, even affectionately with the daily help, the driver and other people who work around the household, also wishing them when they come in and bidding them goodbye for the day, etc. Since being that way comes naturally to you and in your culture, you don't need to be apologetic about it. If your kids are picking up on the local tone and attitude, I think you should unhesitatingly correct them. You can explain to them that they do not need to 'copy' the local way in this matter, and in fact should not.

If this leads to a conversation where your kids then ask you if this friend or that aunty-uncle are bad people for talking that way to their staff, and you want to side-step labelling anything good or bad, you can say that it's not for you to judge. But by your insistence that things are done differently in your home and when your kids visit other homes, it will become clear to your kids that this is the preferred behaviour.

You may find that kids visiting your home will also pick up on this and modify their own way of speaking to their staff.

Other people and youngsters in your situation have even faced resistance or ridicule from local people for 'chit-chatting with the servants' in the homes that they visit. You can smilingly bat off such criticism if it comes your way, if you don't want to debate it out with anyone.

Dos and Don'ts

- Promptly correct your children if you think they are being rude to your domestic staff and taking a supercilious approach towards them.
- Be kind, even affectionate to your servants, drivers etc, wishing them politely etc. If your neightbours are not following a similar attitude, explain to your children that it does not work like that in your house.
- If you set an example, where you are civil and kind towards your staff, it not only sets the preferred tone of behaviour for your kids, even other children around will learn from it.

I for

Idolizing

Your child needs the ordinary, steady time with you rather than any 'quality time' which packs in too many things and leaves your kid too dazzled to appreciate down-to-earth relationships.

Prashant is a thirty-seven-year-old doctor. His seven-year-old son idolizes him and expects a lot from him. Since Prashant gets very little time with his son, he indulges him so much whenever they spend time together that he doesn't listen to his mother or grandmother, and pays no attention to their efforts to play with him or involve him in other activities. Everything for him—fun, entertainment, outings, even studies—is dependent on his dad's availability. Prashant needs to get the message across to his son that he is not superman.

Sometimes children build fantasies around a parent, particularly one who is not present a lot. Perhaps to make up for the limited time that he spends with his son, Prashant is 'dazzling' him with his company and spending what people like to call 'quality time' with him, which usually means an overdose of toys, games, jokes, treats, excitement, interaction, all concentrated in very little time. This becomes a heightened experience for the child, like eating too much sugar and feeling that rush.

When a child associates unbridled fun with one parent, and rules and chores with all the other adults in his life, it gives him unrealistic and lopsided notions. And so a parent like Prashant becomes Superman, someone who swoops out of the sky, does impossibly great things, and leaves in a swoosh! No wonder the child is finding it difficult to enjoy the more steady, regular, and available on-the-ground relationships with the other family members.

Kids need more good old ordinary time rather than the so-called quality time with their parents. Quality time is a concept that overworked parents have coined, not one that children relate to. So we end up providing them some sort of 'highly concentrated dose' of our company and experiences. Of course it is better than spending no-time at all with your kids, but quality time is a highly over-rated concept, and has a very limited role to play in your child's life, if your idea of 'quality' is concentrated excitement.

For instance, a child doing his homework while you read quietly in the other room—available to him if he needs, but not constantly interacting with him—is ordinary time. When you are available to your kids, but not necessarily fully engaged with them is very precious to your children.

Assured, steady involvement rather than an overdose of 'quality' inputs is one of the cornerstones of parenting, and nothing can change that, whichever way you slice it.

Lifestyles and career choices of the last fifty years may have forced us all to think up 'quality time', and it may work in a limited way, maybe in corporate situations but not with friendships, marriages, parent–child relationships or any other significant human interaction.

Dos and Don'ts

- Quality time is an overrated concept. Avoid making up for lost time with kids by dazzling them with short-term activities.
- Give 'ordinary time' to your kids, which means being available to kids but not necessarily fully engaged with them.

Interviews

Children tend to pick up vibes from their parents, so if a parent is nervous, so will the child be. Interviews can be a bit daunting, however as the parents should try to maintain their calm if they want their child to be calm too. Often kids freeze and are unable to perform on the 'big day'. The better approach is to not treat the interview as some kind of impending doom, and let the child develop social skills in casual settings.

Aruna's daughter is five years old and is going to appear for pre-primary school interviews. While she is bright and knows her pre-school stuff, she tends to get into a shell when she meets strangers and does not talk much. When Aruna asks her some potential interview questions, she gives the right answers most of the time and says she doesn't know when she can't answer the question. Aruna does not believe in putting any kind of pressure on her and would like to boost her daughter's self confidence. How can she go about preparing her to talk confidently at interviews?

While it's great that Aruna does not want to put pressure

on her daughter, she must also be aware that children pick up on a parent's tensions or stress, and Aruna is already tensed about this. However, having said that, you do have some real anxiety about how she will perform, given that a lot depends on this interview. Why not shift the focus away from the interview completely and subtly begin to work on her social skills? Recruit a few of your friends and neighbours to engage her in conversations, asking her questions, drawing her out a little from her shell. This could be small casual exchanges, and not mock interviews. For the next few weeks, you could have more people over, go out with a friend or acquaintance along with your daughter for lunch, and set up other such situations that will gently push her into interacting with new people.

Do not define the problem in front of her. If you keep telling her that she 'knows everything but must learn to talk to the interviewer', it will only make her more self-conscious and anxious. She may then end up clinging even more nervously to you during the interview. Avoid defining the problem in front of her to other adults too. You may end up making a 'self-fulfilling prophecy' kind of situation, where she acts out exactly what you fear that she will do during the interview.

The sad fact is that many schools are so overwhelmed by the number of applications, that they need any small reason to disqualify a child. Keep this in mind, and have a Plan B ready, so that you as well as your child don't enter the interview process with a huge burden on your shoulders. That in itself makes kids freeze up.

Think about working on your child's socializing process more as a life skill that will serve her well later when she has to relate and engage with people outside the family unit. Whether there is an interview looming or not, it's something we have to give our children—the ability to let go of our hands a little, and trust another adult.

Dos and Don'ts

- Recruit a few of your close friends and neighbours to interact with your child so that he/she eases up and is not overwhelmed about the school interview process. It would then seem like natural progression.

- Do not define the problem of her inability to perform or your own worry in front of the child. It will make her nervous and self-conscious

J for

❧

Joint Families

Making comparisons between kids mostly tends to backfire, as it fosters feelings of jealousy and ill will. Adults in the family must resist this tendency as much as possible.

The Danis live in a semi-joint family (various related couples and their kids in different apartments in one building). In all, there are three couples and four children. The parents have consciously decided never to compare the kids with each other on any level. However, the grandparents, an aunt and uncle and the nanny tend to do this a lot. When the concerned parents have tried to talk this out, the caregivers say that the parents are being too fussy and that in fact this is a way to get kids to do better. As the elders and the domestic helps are the care-providers throughout the day, since the parents are all at work, their influence on the kids is strong. How can the working parents drive their point home better, and how do they not let it affect their kids?

Comparing children is a common quick-fix strategy to get kids to complete tasks and chores and to behave. Some degree of this kind of a thing can also be used as a tool to motivate kids. For example, phrases such as 'See how well he's eaten his food', or 'Look at how nicely she's done her homework'. This can spur the child onto complete a task that he/she has been stalling. So a hard and fast rule is not something that can be easily followed when there are several kids around and people who have to take care of them through the day using various devices and techniques. Moreover, the care-givers in such households are usually older people and domestic help, and would probably be fairly set in their ways.

However, comparisons are of limited use and can work negatively. Most children react to comparisons with some sort of defence mechanism, such as ignoring what you're saying, or coming up with a sullen and unreasonable response like 'Well she does it because she's stupid', or 'She's finished her homework because she's a goody-goody'. In such cases, your comparison has not only *not* worked, it has also pushed the child further away from what you want him to do. Moreover, this could cause unhealthy rivalry between the kids.

What you need to look out for is that one (the angelic, obedient one) child is not being held up as a shining example all the time. This really sets kids against each other, both the 'good' kid as well as the ones being pulled up suffer from this kind of constant, one-way comparison. If this is happening, you'll need to talk to your care-providers and request them to not do this too often.

The other thing that you can do is to request them to try to compare each child with his or her own best behaviour. It is always much more positive and effective to compare a child *with his own potential*. 'How well you tidied up yesterday', or 'How nicely you finish your vegetables usually', would be more motivating strategies, and you could suggest that these be used.

The bottom line is that the comparison-tool has to be constructive and should never target a child's sense of self—comparisons about physical appearance would then be a complete no-no, as they do nothing but create anxiety, embarrassment, and low self-worth.

Dos and Don'ts

- It is always more positive and effective when comparison is made with a child's own potential.
- Comparing kids with each other on physical traits is an absolute no-no.

Junk Food

Getting your kids not to dig into packets of potato chips and other junk food when their friends bring them along is no doubt tough. Work around the problem and come up with interesting food options that 'deglamourizes' junk.

Every time Mita's neighbour's kid comes over, all the rules of her home go out of the window. For instance, he'll bring over a 2-litre bottle of Pepsi, large bags of chips, and other junk food that Mita's kids are only allowed in limited quantities once a week. She tried to explain this to him and his mother but to no effect. Mita is looking for ways that she can control the snacking habit of the neighbour's out-of-control, but sweet and affectionate child when he comes into her home without being a party-pooper in her children's eyes who adore him and are his best friends.

It is always tough to keep your child abstained from things that his or her friends are indulging in. The truth is that an over-indulgent kid is a product of lazy, path-of-least resistance parenting. And you will encounter this at various stages of your own 'parenting career'. Right now it's about colas and fried foods, in an older age group it will be about pocket money, clothes, late nights, driving the car, boyfriends, girlfriends…and a hundred other things that the kid next door may be allowed to do, which just does not fit in with your idea of parenting.

Now disciplining this neighbour's kid is not really your mandate.

So here's what you'll have to do. Firstly, you'll have to take your kids into confidence and plan a kind of gambit. Sit them down and have a chat in which you may have to subtly indicate to them that the neighbour's 'poor' kid seems not to have access to more interesting foods and activities. Come up with a plan with your kids to put together some fun food and drink (as defined by you in your home) when the neighbour's kid comes over. If you have the time and energy to do it, it will be well worth it. If you're not inclined to cooking, buy some kiddies-in-the-kitchen kind of cookbooks, and let them muck around a bit—chikki, nimbu-pani, bhel, home-flipped burgers—there's plenty of decent kid food around that you can entice them with.

The next time boy-next-door shows up armed with his favourite food, you can all look dismayed (acting skills to be honed here) and then tell him and the parent to bring over something less boring when he comes to play. Throw in a smiling suggestion that if they can't, you'll be happy to provide it. Basically you're working at de-glamourizing the junk that he's addicted to eating and bringing into your house. I know this sounds crafty and manipulative but, well, so be it.

The other slightly lamer option is to negotiate with your neighbour that at least the quantities of this stuff that he gets are reduced. Half a litre cola distributed in small glasses, and a few chips should keep them happy.

You have to be very firm about this whole issue and brook no arguments. Declare your home a cola-and-chip-free zone on some days, and simply stick to it. I know it doesn't feel good to always be the resident dragoness, but you and your kids can't be held hostage in your own home by a visitor's unhealthy eating habits.

Dos and Don'ts

- Be creative and entice your kids with healthier but tasty food options, which then makes the junk food appear boring.
- Negotiate with your neighbour to allow less junk food to be let into your house.
- If nothing works, approach the matter a little bluntly for the sake of your kids' health.

K for

Kowtowing

Kids who bend backwards for their friends are ironically not very liked, in spite of them going out of their way not to offend anyone. Parents must find ways to build the child's self-esteem, so that he/she feels confident to do the right thing without fear of rejection.

Ragini's fifteen-year-old daughter is the opposite of rude. She is far too nice, and gets caught up in doing things that she doesn't want to do because she is unable to say no. This involves all sorts of favours like dropping and picking up people, rerouting the family car on her way to classes, lending books that she never gets back, giving notes when she needs to study from them too, lending her jewellery etc. Now she even goes on outings or parties that she is not particularly interested in or which she has a problem with, where boys and girls pair off and get physical. She prefers to argue with Ragini and go, rather than say no to her friends, even if she really doesn't want to go. Her parents have been telling her that this way she will be taken for granted.

This fifteen-year-old is a pleaser in the making. Ragini

is right in raising a red flag on this behaviour. While the spirit of co-operation and helpfulness is something that we all try to inculcate in our kids, there is also an issue of boundaries—of being able to form the outlines and content of one's personality without fearing being 'disliked' or 'rejected'. The problem with the pleaser personality is that people around tend to take a pleaser for granted and will continue to push the boundaries. Ironically then, the pleaser is not genuinely liked by her friends but is only seen as 'useful'. This is something that you would need to sensitively point out to her. Many parents in this situation tend to mock and angrily declare 'They just want your car, and not your company' or some such statement, in a bid to open their child's eyes to the situation.

Sometimes kids become people–pleasing young adults if one or both parents have been extremely exacting and have laid a lot of emphasis on obedience and compliance with a fairly rigid set of family rules. If this is something that has happened in your child's case, you would need to do a considerable amount of interpersonal work between you and her, perhaps with the help of a counsellor. This would involve you learning to let her make and respect some of her decisions, opinions and choices, even in small matters like clothes, tastes, and in bigger issues too. If the above is not the case, and she has not grown up in such an atmosphere, you can also help her to gradually learn to express her feelings, what she wants, and how to stick to it, without fearing rejection.

You could start with helping her outline what she ideally

wants out of a situation. Even if she actually ends up doing what others want, it would be a useful beginning for her to be able to articulate and frame what she really wants or wishes for. After some sessions or weeks of this, the next step would be to help her think through what she fears will or will not happen if she states her own needs or limitations to her friends. This is an important stage for the child to outgrow the people–pleasing mode. Assure her that once she forms clearer boundaries, real friends who respect them will emerge.

Dos and Don'ts

- Encourage her to articulate and outline what she wants in a situation without the fear of rejection.
- Let her think through what she fears will or will not happen if she expresses her opinion or limitations clearly to her friends.

L for

Loner

Many kids are painfully shy of any social interaction involving family functions, festivals, etc. This is not uncommon, and with a little sensitivity and patience, the child can be eased into talking and engaging with others.

Dara is an intelligent, affectionate boy. However, he hates social functions, so much so that his mother Ava dreads having to take him out to any of them. His father travels for work and rarely attends such functions. Dara, his mother says, misbehaves in every possible manner when it is time to go to some social function. He whines, sulks, takes forever to get ready, and then at the function itself, he displays a range of socially awkward behaviours—refusing to let go of his mom's hand or some part of her clothing even when she is seated next to him, repeating 'mummy' many times over, and having nothing to say when she asks him what he wants. He will simply not answer polite queries from people, pull exasperated faces, insist he is hungry and when served food, he says that the food is not to his liking, refusing to say thank you for presents that anyone gives him, and so on. Needless to say, this behaviour embarrasses his mother deeply. Elders as well as children end up teasing Dara for his actions and that makes him behave even worse! When they return home, he says 'sorry' to his mother, and she feels that he genuinely means it. She has tried punishing him, ignoring him, as well as 'bribing' him with different things but she is not able to change his behaviour. Should Ava simply not take him to such functions and also lose out on these outings herself?

There are many children who truly hate such occasions; they find absolutely no reason that they should subject themselves to dressing neatly and watching people milling about! Having said that, of course, attending such events is part of the socialization process, and all of us have to learn to put up with social situations that don't interest us, but from which we may ultimately learn or get something and give something in the form of enjoying the company of other human beings.

In this case, Dara feels trapped and threatened in these situations, and is very insecure about his mom's focus being away from him and temporarily on other people. Perhaps it's also because she and him are together a lot, safe and cozy as a family of two most times. So when they attend social occasions with a lot of people around, Dara finds the transition extremely difficult and abhorrent.

A good way to bring in the outside world gradually may be to take a child on an outing with just a couple of other friends (yours and his), or have a couple of people over along with their children, more often. Then the bigger occasions may become easier for him to deal with.

Another strategy could be that you let your reluctant child not come for some of the functions, leaving him or her in the care of someone, if that is an option. For the next function that you do take him to, you could tell him, in advance, a little about the people that he will be meeting—some nice trait or anecdote about an aunt or uncle, some interesting achievement or characteristic that would interest him (for instance, is there someone who paraglides, or whistles well, or keeps fish, or is a dog lover, or is a mountaineer, or anything that a boy of his age would get interested in), it may hold his attention when he's there. This would also help your child think of some of the people he is meeting as individuals, and not as a threatening and boring mass of humanity that takes his mother away from him. You could also find ways to assure him that you enjoy such occasions and want his support in letting you have fun. Convey that it doesn't mean that you are switched off from him at all during this time. If you can get across the feeling that your enjoying can make both of you happy, by putting you in a good mood, etc., that would be a useful line of thought to open up for him.

Perhaps the absence of a father at such places makes Dara, and kids like him, feel that these are all mom/women's activities. It's important for the father of such a child to make it for a few of these social/family functions, and let the son see how he enjoys them and engages with people too. Another device could be to find an understanding and trustworthy friend/relative, preferably male, who takes him under his wing during the function and lets him 'hang with the men', and he may feel less oppressed and out-of-sync.

Keep an eye out for signs of extreme restlessness and poor attention span or trouble making friends in school hours. If so, the social behaviour is something that could be part of a larger behavioural pattern, and would need to be assessed and tested by a professional.

Dos and Don'ts

- ✎ Tell him a few interesting things about the people you will be meeting. It might trigger his fancy and he won't feel averse to meeting people.
- ✎ Look out for signs in the child that could point to larger social and behavioural problems.

M for

Mother Tongue

Embarrassment about one parent being unable to speak 'pristine' English is something kids have to be guided to get over with. It comes from the attitudes that are all around, and this kind of snobbery is best tackled head-on.

Mohana is from an English-medium school and her husband studied in Hindi schools. He subsequently joined world-class institutions of higher-education, and today is well-placed and comfortable in global situations. However, his English has a bit of a regional Indian accent, and he mispronounces some words. While Mohana has never thought it is any kind of problem, their eleven-year-old Dia has begun to correct her father all the time, and seems to be almost embarrassed about him. She recently told her mother that she should not bring her father to the PTA meeting. Both the parents do not like this attitude of hers and have explained to her that it is no big deal if he gets a few words wrong. Mohana is now afraid that this is going to cause a rift between them, because the father too has now begun to get self-conscious around his daughter.

Children of Dia's age are at the beginning of that phase where there is a slightly exaggerated sense of not wanting to stick out, feeling watched by others, being afraid of teasing and ridicule, wanting desperately to blend in. Part of this means that they are mildly to acutely embarrassed by their parents. This awkwardness about ones parents can be for not even any apparent reason, or for reasons that seem minor and baseless to us as adults. Since their own egos are so wafer-thin, going towards adolescence, every little 'variation' on how they think things 'should be' are seen as threatening to their own dignity!

The reason that Dia is feeling socially awkward—her father's accent when he speaks English—is an issue that her parents rightly believe needs to be tackled and put to rest. Firstly, because it is her father, and secondly, to slowly but subtly weed out notions that rise out of meaningless snobbery from a growing child's mind. It is the kind of snobbery that many grown people exhibit, and it cuts them off from connecting with a whole lot of good and valuable people and building relationships outside their little social boxes! Perhaps the school that she goes to and her peer group too are feeding some of her notions.

Parents in similar situations could deal with it on a few different levels. At one level, her father could play along a bit and take on some of the corrections; he could also ask her to write down five words that he mispronounces, which bother her the most and promise to work on them. Yes, it's always good to say something the way it is supposed to be said, to speak a language well, however, you must send out the subtle message that at some level it truly does not matter, and that he functions perfectly well the way he speaks currently. The correction is being made to please her.

While you are on the subject of language, perhaps you could also put some pressure on her to speak her own mother tongue well, so that this notion in her mind, that 'English is superior to all other languages' is also subtly modified, and she learns to respect her father's language skills in Hindi.

You will have to show that you are both utterly comfortable in your own shoes and accents. Cutting a little closer to the bone of the issue, you could find ways for her to see how well her dad is doing in his field, how well-liked he is socially, and how none of this has anything to do with how he speaks. She is a little too young to overload too much information on and lecturing her on the subject, but you could find ways to keep up the line of thought, including talking about how many people with smooth and impeccable English accents can be quite deficient on many other levels.

Dos and Don'ts

- ❧ The parent could play along and take on some of the corrections. But all the same, reiterate subtly that it does not really matter and it is being done only to please her.
- ❧ Put some pressure on the child to get her own mother tongue right first, so that the view of English being superior to regional languages is automatically questioned.

Multi-tasking

When busy multi-tasking working parents come home only to plug in their laptops or get on the phone while sitting with their kids, it needs to be identified as a family communication crisis.

In a family of working parents, when the mother, Ayesha, comes home, she has no choice but to multi-task. She has children to supervise, and also clients in another continent to connect with. This makes the kids extremely resentful, seeing their mother talking on the phone or using her laptop, even though she sits at the dining table and watches over their homework or even plays a game with them at the same time. One of her children has even recently refused to play or talk with her if she is on the phone or the computer. Ayesha feels that she has no choice, and her children must understand. She also believes that it is a lesson in multi-tasking for the kids, something that they will soon have to learn themselves. Is she right?

While multi-tasking on some fronts is inevitable, multi-tasking in home–work situations is turning out to be a way of doing many things badly—multi-failing. And relationships are the first casualty!

Since the kids in this situation are clearly protesting, could their mother consider this: promise them that she will not switch on the laptop or pick up the phone after she comes home from work, through their dinner, and till they sleep at 9 pm? Another parent says she would come home, chat with her kids or play a game or even read for them from a book, but have her phone plugged into her ear and her laptop open at the dining table, into which she would peep, chat online and scan FB. If her kids called for her attention she would say, 'But I'm HERE!', and would continue talking work with someone or stay networked. She would be unable to do that fully either, as she had to tell these people that she had to get back to the kids.

We are in the midst of an epidemic (and I use this word seriously) of hollow communication. Sure we have lots of people in our lives, but we're giving nothing but casual updates and photo uploads to these people most of the times, and while we're doing this, many of us are ignoring the real people in our homes and lives. There is a serious threat to our ability to read our own as well as our dear ones' moods, needs, fears and hopes, in this feverish need to stay 'connected' all the time. Perhaps it's time to firmly restrict use of our phones and computers, and re-learn to just be with ourselves and our families in a more real and ultimately much more fulfilling way.

Dos and Don'ts

- Restrict the use of phones and computers at home and make sure to be emotionally and physically available to your near and dear ones.
- Come up with a mutually agreed no-electronics time within the family, whether you have small kids or teenagers in the family.

N for

❧

Naming

Giving children unusual names is one thing, but saddling them with names that are easily up for ridicule and mockery is doing a grave disservice to a child. The name may have religious or spiritual significance to the parent, but it is the child who has to live with it.

Aarti's sister has named her child a very obscure name from the scriptures. The word sounds odd, funny, and near-obscene in English and looks really bad when written down. The baby is a few months old, but already the other kids laugh at the name and go on chanting it because it is very amusing. You can imagine how this is going to get worse when the child starts going to school. The child's mother says that the meaning of the name is suggested by her spiritual leader, and its meaning is so beautiful and appropriate that she will teach her daughter to be proud of it. Aarti has been urging her to find another name with a similar meaning and better social acceptability.

The Internet is full of sites about parents naming kids that range from the odd to the downright ridiculous. People then quote 'studies' about how kids with odd names do well, or there are other studies which say that kids with odd names fail at what they do, etc. It all seems pretty cruel to saddle a child with a name that is not only odd but 'funny and obscene' too. Surely there is no need to get so attached to the significance of a name if it is going to set your child up for teasing, mockery and ridicule. A child can be taught to live with and even be proud of an 'unusual' name but if you know that you are sending your child into the distinctly odd and laughable zone, then that is nothing but placing a millstone around a child's neck.

Aarti's sister's faith in her spiritual leader does not have to be manifested in the child's name necessarily. And surely this leader should be made aware that it is as if he is playing some cosmic joke on the child by suggesting a name that will be so embarrassing for the child to live with.

Many people who were christened with odd names that invited teasing and derision when they were growing up, say that they waited impatiently till they could jettison the name legally, or resorted to 'giving themselves' a pet name, and going to great lengths to hide the real name. With the world becoming something of a global village, today it is not easy to live with a name that means something terrible or funny in another culture, since various cultures do intersect often now. It's not that parents need to consider how it sounds or means in many languages, but if as you say it sounds bad in English itself, which is spoken all over the world, and in this country too, then I would say she really needs to reconsider her decision about naming her baby.

Dos and Don'ts

- ✑ Giving an unusual name to your child is alright, but if it falls into the zone of laughable or obscene, it is advisable to change it.
- ✑ Be practical and do not attach too much value to the significance of the name, especially if it is odd enough and will embarrass your child when he/she grows up.

Nastiness

When we catch our kids being nasty and insensitive, we need to put in place a multi-pronged approach to getting them to reflect, unlearn some of their attitudes, and learn empathy.

Mrs Kapur was shocked to discover that her daughter and two friends in school (both in class 8) were teasing a boy who is visually impaired. He has a severe squint and poor vision, but manages well in school. She just could not understand how and why it happened but was told that her daughter and friends began to call him all sorts of names and when he retaliated with some name-calling of his own, they began to spread tales that he stared at their chests. The school the kids go to believes in a disability-inclusive mix of students, and Mr and Mrs Kapur were shocked at her insensitivity. They were punished at school, but her daughter seemed quite unashamed and even broke out into giggles while telling her parents what it was that she called him. They are distraught and feel ashamed about their daughter's behaviour and just don't know the way forward with her.

Mr and Mrs Kapur's horror and embarrassment at their

daughter's behaviour is quite understandable. Right now their daughter seems in a mood to not be receptive at all to any chastisement or any appeal to her emotional intelligence in this matter.

What they, as well as the school, could do on an ongoing basis is to involve a counsellor or person working in the field of emotional and social intelligence to come up with a programme for young people to be empathetic and emotionally intelligent. It is important that her parents not position this as 'being more charitable' or 'full of pity and sympathy'—this kind of an attitude only further alienates children from those with special needs.

The idea of disability-inclusion in schools is not just for other kids to learn how to include and work with the disabled, but also for the disabled to be integrated in the hurly-burly of ordinary school life—bullying, teasing, and everything else included. So it is not that the Kapurs need to teach their daughter to treat the visually impaired child with 'kid gloves'—that would be artificial and unfair to him too, what their daughter needs to learn is where to draw the line with teasing, that is, when it goes too far and becomes cruel.

Parents whose children are showing traits of nastiness should talk to their children about what it is that he or she doesn't like about the boy that they tease. Two things could emerge—firstly, the child being teased has some traits or attitudes that irritates the teaser, which has nothing to do with his or her disability; in that case her parents could tell her that it is okay to not like him, but not okay to use his disability as something to trouble him with. Secondly, the child genuinely has not developed the ability to be respectful and empathetic of someone's weaknesses. If the latter is the case then his or her parents and the school will have to work on building in this important personality component. It's best done without lecturing and punishing (as described in this case, she seems to find even that amusing), and better to work with a professional who will find ways to develop the idea of empathy in the child.

Making kids empathetic and sensitive to others is an on-going process and you have to find the right medium through which to do it. Her parents can start with having her watch educational and inspirational videos on the Internet (for example, TED talks by or on people with disabilities who speak about their lives, their fantastic achievements, the supportive and loving people around them). A professional who works with fostering emotional intelligence can come up with many age-appropriate techniques and material that can be used either in the school as a programme with a bunch of kids together or with individual children.

Dos and Don'ts

- Don't teach kids to pity or 'do charity' to kids with disabilities. However, do teach them to account for the disability with sensitivity.
- If you feel your child genuinely lacks the ability to empathize and be sensitive to others, you could perhaps take the help of a professional counsellor.

Notions

Why burden and limit kids with our pre-conceived prejudices under the guise of giving career advice? We do them a big disservice when we colour their thoughts about some work being 'better' than something else.

For three years now, nine-year-old Pranav has been fascinated with pilots—their work, uniforms, helmets, and all things associated with them. However, his parents, both scientists and academics, have begun to harp on how he should now be interested in the principle of things and study aeronautics or physics, rather than in being a pilot or 'wasting time' on playing make-believe with model aircraft, etc. Pranav's aunt noticed that he has simply stopped talking about the subject now, because, as she guesses rightly, he does not feel good about being lectured and his pilot fascination simply being dismissed by his parents.

Surely it is really too early to overwhelm a nine-year-old by shooting down his current fascination and trying to replace it with notions about what he 'should' be planning to do. Moreover, Pranav's parents must know that no pilot gets to fly a plane without knowing a lot about the principles of aeronautics and physics in the first place! Why not simply let the child enjoy and indulge in his interest; it's not like he has to make a choice tomorrow, and it is a disservice to any profession to talk about 'lower' and 'higher' aspects.

Aruna faced a similar attitudinal bias. She caters for parties from her home kitchen, and makes a good living out of it, while her husband and his siblings and parents are a family of scientists. When she heard her daughter's grandparents once saying to her jokingly that she should study hard, or she will end up 'frying samosas', Aruna could ignore the jibe, but felt that in itself, it is not right to teach a child that some work is 'intelligent' and 'brainy' and some work is to be dismissed as 'low brow'.

For all our talk about the dignity of labour, mindless prejudices are well-entrenched. People from the educated classes can be rather arrogant and narrow in their response to work that is not 'intellect-driven'!

To teach a child to disdain any kind of work is wrong and limiting. And to coach a child to belittle or be ashamed of her mother's occupation is plain harmful. Children must be guided by family members to do everything wholeheartedly, enjoy all kinds of experiences, and respect every kind of profession.

Dos and Don'ts

- ⤷ Don't be overly anxious about your child's career aspirations. Let him or her indulge his fantasies for now.
- ⤷ Never demean any vocation or prejudice your child's mind. Guide your children to do everything whole-heartedly and enjoy their experiences.

Night-outs

❦

We have to come up with strategies and arrangements so that our teenagers can go out, enjoy themselves, and yet be safe from drunken drivers, and other unsavoury elements that could prey on them.

Meenaxi's daughters (seventeen and eighteen) have been asking to go out at night for movies, plays or for parties, either at someone's house or in a restobar or lounge, with other girls. While the parents don't want to be repressive, they are not ready to send them out at night on their own. They live in one of the smaller cities, which is moderately safe, but speeding vehicles and other such hazards at night are a concern, and there are some lonely stretches on the way home which could prove unsafe. How do parents today let teenagers have some harmless fun and yet be safe?

This is a tough one, and something many city parents are trying to figure out. Yes, you do want your teenagers to experience that teenage fun of going out at night on their own but there definitely are valid concerns about safety, not just from unsavoury elements, but also from people who are drunk driving, speeding, and jumping red lights at night—a very common feature of the night-life, particularly in cities like the one they stay in. One of the key things is knowing where your children are going and what vehicle they are going to use. You need to ascertain whether your children or their friends are careful drivers. If you or one of their friends has a known, dependable chauffeur, then it makes things a little easier.

What some parents choose to do, is this: allow them to go for a clear-cut programme—a movie or a show, then dinner and back home. A night out which involves moving through too many locations is a source of worry to parents, and should be avoided if possible. Of course there has got to be a curfew time. Anything after midnight is iffy, as all cops will tell you!

Some parents prefer, taking turns with other parents, to take the teenagers out themselves. Not that you should muscle in on their outing. It works something like this—they go to their movie/dinner/show on their own. A couple of hours later, the parents go out themselves, to a nearby pub or restaurant or whatever it is you like to and can do in the area where your teenagers are. (Of course you don't go to the same place that they are in!). You then pick them all up and drop them to their homes. This way, all the parents know that their kids are semi-supervised, and not finding their way home on their own at night. The teenagers might protest at this suggestion, which sounds suspiciously like they are being chaperoned, but it really is the best way to let them go off on their own without you worrying till they return. Teenagers protest that they now have cell phones and can call you if they are stuck or in any kind of trouble but ideally you should still assess if a place is safe, if the people are okay, if the ride home is dependable, etc. because going out at night is a new thing for them. It makes sense to come up with some arrangement like the one outlined above, so that you're not playing bodyguard to your teenagers, but are at least just a shout away.

Dos and Don'ts

- Find out who is driving the car and if they safe, dependable drivers.
- A curfew is a must for night outings.
- Make your teenagers stick to a clear-cut programme, a movie and a dinner, etc., so that there is not too much moving around at night.
- You could possibly take turns with other parents to accompany the children. You could be in the same area where the children are, without chaperoning them per se. And when they are done, you can safely drop them home.

O for

Obesity

Urban Indian kids are becoming victims of poor eating and lifestyle habits. Quiet and steady change in the home diet and exercise routines can keep obesity at bay.

Chitra has an eleven-year-old son who was a chubby baby and toddler, but now he is heading to be an overweight youngster. He gets teased quite a bit about his weight, including by his teachers sometimes. Most of her friends and family tend to laugh it off and say that he is just 'healthy'. Nowadays he makes jokes about his own weight, which is something Chitra is not comfortable with. How does she help him cope with the teasing, and at the same time get into better shape? Her husband thinks the teasing is okay and that the teasing may motivate the boy to do something about his weight.

Contrary to some perceptions that chubby children are cheerful and always clowning around, the fact is that obese kids lack self-esteem and are often socially awkward and maladjusted. This poor self-image, in turn leads to a vicious cycle which they make up by overeating, joking about their weight, or being aggressive, but inside almost every overweight child is a vulnerable, hurt, and an unhappy person.

The words used to tease may change over the years from 'polson' to 'tuntun' to 'jaadi' to 'motu' to 'tubby' to 'sumo' and the likes, but the fact remains that a fat child is often picked on and mocked mercilessly right through his or her school years.

While obesity in children has not reached epidemic proportions, as in the West, we do see an alarming rise of obesity and related disorders in the urban Indian child population.

With children leading increasingly sedentary lives even during recreation time—in front of the TV or a computer—and a rise in the consumption of fast food, the last decade has seen child obesity as a growing urban Indian phenomenon. We are firmly in a world where most commercially available snacks and fast food contribute hugely to obesity and nothing to nutrition. While this trend is unlikely to change in the near future, there is quite a lot that we can do in our homes to ensure that our children have a healthy upbringing. Changes in lifestyle and food choices will go a long way in preventing our kids from becoming overweight, undernourished, and unhappy.

Urban Indians have also started buying tremendous amounts of food, and stocking the house with unending choices, turning it into a mini supermarket. This automatically encourages kids and adults to snack and use food as 'time pass' or entertainment. Eating while doing some other activities like watching TV, playing games on the computer, talking on the phone has become very common nowadays. While it's not easy to not stock your larder, it is a good idea to make your main meals, as well as a big snack, into a sit-down meal for the whole family. This way everyone gets to chat and let their hair down without their attention being held by something else. This is conscious eating, and not casual 'popping things into your mouth' kind of indiscriminate snacking.

For those who are grossly overweight, and have a family history of obesity, the help of doctors, dieticians and fitness experts is the main recourse. For kids who are marginally overweight, there is so much that we can do at home, by making small but significant changes in eating habits, attitudes to food, and other routines. For weight loss, have small targets, and every time the child passes the milestone, reward him or her with a piece of clothing or some such thing that he can now get into. You will find that weight loss brings its own best rewards in terms of better self esteem, better school performance, and a happier disposition.

Dos and Don'ts

- ❧ Avoid taunting, joking or teasing as a part of your strategy to get a child to exercise or eat less.
- ❧ Request (or insist) that the teachers in school don't refer to his weight.
- ❧ Cut down on bakery products—bread, cakes, biscuits, confectionary and the like. Enjoy them once in a while, and look for whole-wheat alternatives for everyday snacks.

- 🔊 Simply say no to aerated drinks. Do not stock them at home, and allow one, at the most, once in a week. Offer alternatives through summer, like chaas, nimbu paani, coconut water, kokum sarbat, and other such choices.
- 🔊 Take a family walk after dinner; if possible, walk kids to school or part of the way.
- 🔊 Insist on some outdoor games at least twice a week.
- 🔊 Encourage kids to sit on the floor when they play board or card games, work at craft, drawing and the like.
- 🔊 Above all, don't make his or her weight a 'big family problem' to be discussed with anyone you meet or who drops by.

Older Parents

Choosing to have a child later than the norm, is now not that unusual. Older parents have their share of anxieties and challenges, but it need not be traumatic.

Kala and Shrini are in their late-forties. Busy with careers and multiple city changes, they chose to have their child late. He's just five now and the centre of their universe. But they worry that they need to prepare him for a time, maybe as soon as twenty years hence, when they may not be around or may not be active. Also, his friends' parents are much younger, and they feel the mismatch at times. They don't have much of a larger family to fall back on, though they have a close-knit friends' circle whose children are mostly older than their son. Both Kala and Shrini feel that they need to in some way include more significant adults in this child's life.

The most pertinent question that older parents ask is: after us, what? Firstly, today no longer do we have to assume that old age equals ill health and incapacity. You could quite be a sprightly and energetic parent till late into your life. And death is a famous prankster, so older parents like Kala and Shrini have to necessarily assume that you won't be around for your child after his twenties.

Secondly, it is also the quality of time that you spend with him that has to count, and this will last him well beyond your lifetime. A child brought up in a secure and loving environment by middle-aged parents is more likely to be emotionally anchored and prepared for different situations, and has a big advantage over any child that has an unstable home with young parents. While physical and financial support and being there 'long enough' is a primary concern for older parents, so much can be gifted to your child in terms of being emotionally present. Which is, needless to say, not to mean that older parents cosset and spoil their children, but provide far-reaching emotional security in mature and well-thought-out ways.

Whether you are a young or older parent, children should be encouraged to make bonds with other significant adults, favourite aunts and uncles, godparents, older cousins. So many of us as adults have deep and sustaining relationships with aunts, uncles, or friends of parents, well after their parents may have passed on. That is another kind of wealth that you can provide your child. And this comes first from yourself investing in the friendships that you have. Secondly, older parents have a greater responsibility to remain fit, physically, emotionally and financially, towards which you should work steadily and positively.

As an older parent, you should avoid at any point talking about 'we won't be around forever you know' kind of conversations with your children, even in later years. Also avoid referring to yourself as the 'oldies' and talking about the youngness of other parents compared to yourself, etc. Your age is simply a fact, and your children will grow up with that fact. Moreover, your situation is much more common these days.

Late parents obviously have not entered parenthood casually or by default. It is a well thought out and composed decision. They need to maintain the same equanimity and self-assurance when they are beset by anxieties, small and big, involving their child's future.

Dos and Don'ts

- ❧ Look at the positives. The quality time you spend with your child will last a lifetime. And the secure and loving home you give him/her will be an advantage over children from unstable families of young parents.
- ❧ Old age no more equals ill health. You can very well be as agile as young parents. All the same middle-aged parents have a greater responsibility to be fit and healthy and should work towards this.
- ❧ Encourage your children to make bonds with other significant adults, favourite aunts and uncles, godparents, older cousins. This is a valuable asset to have, something which parents must cultivate from the start.

Over-preparation

Avoid being a hard taskmaster while overseeing your child's studies. Some breathing space enables children to learn, retain, and perform better in exam situations.

Twelve-year-old Geetika's mother has a common complaint. In spite of rigorous coaching at home, her daughter loses crucial marks in her school exams due to carelessness. Often, she copies the sums wrong and hence gets the answers wrong. Sometimes she just forgets to label diagrams and loses marks this way. Geetika's mother is a stickler in these matters and gets her daughter to study at least five hours every day. And during these sessions, Geetika performs perfectly. But in school, to her mother's dismay, she doesn't seem to apply herself too well. Not only does she make silly mistakes, what irritates her mother is that she does not even show the inclination to check her answer sheets and spot the errors she keeps repeating.

Perhaps all these are signs that the child is being 'over-prepared' at home. Children whose parents work with them on their studies all the time, tend to do this—they are on their toes at home, where they are being watched constantly, so they study hard and do all the right things, but there is no real learning or retention possibly. Once they're away from the home atmosphere, they tend to 'relax' in school, when they become part of a mass and nobody is breathing down their necks. Since the respective parent is quite demanding and exacting in the home-study routine, the child manages to perform well with him/her around and in the atmosphere of a great deal of focusing and concentration. However, at school she probably relaxes or even over-relaxes and blanks out, and this results in carelessness.

For a child of this age, marks may not be so very important right now. If the parents can let go a little, and loosen up the home routine, the situation may reverse slowly, and the child will perform better. Right now, the mother is being the taskmaster, while the school is where the daughter can slack off. It should be the other way round. The child is on her toes while writing the exam, and is able to relax a little at home and make some mistakes in the preparatory practices done with parents.

There's another aspect to this too. Geetika's mother says that her daughter doesn't want to or couldn't be bothered to look at the returned answer sheet. Why would she, given that Geetika looks at it in such detail and analyzes what went wrong for her; Geetika is unconsciously playing both ring-master and secretary rolled into one to your child.

Parents in these situations need to step back a little. Perfectionist parents often cut children off from taking responsibility for themselves. Here Geetika knows that her mother is in control and will not just do the studying with her, but even the understanding of what went wrong. In this way, a child ends up staying completely out of the process of learning, retaining, focusing while preparing for the exam, and stays connected to the result and the feedback on her answer paper.

While it is understandable that parents want to stay close to their kids on the homework and studies front, we need to give them the leeway to make mistakes and experience the consequences of those mistakes firsthand. This cannot happen if the parents take the entire onus of studies, exams, and results. Your child has to begin to want to do well on his or her own, and not only because you want it for her.

Dos and Don'ts

- Do not play ring-master to your child and be over-obsessed about her studies. Perfectionist parents, who take on all the onus of studies and exams, often cut off children from taking responsibility themselves.
- Give your child the leeway to make mistakes and experience the consequences of those mistakes.
- Being too stringent and exacting at home can leave children often exhausted and bored to apply themselves in exams.
- Let children derive joy through studies and wish to do well for their own sake.

P for

Parties

Kids' birthday parties can be a source of tension and unhappiness, given the way people are vamping them up into over-the-top events. However, you can still keep it real and enjoy the occasion along with your kids.

Amrita's friend's daughter had her birthday recently. They are a middle-class family, much like Amrita's, but she was shocked at the lavishness of the party, the return gifts, the food, etc. On the way back, Amrita's daughter, who is six and about the same age as the birthday girl, was very quiet. Before going to bed, she turned to her mom and said that she didn't want to celebrate her next birthday because we wouldn't be able to give such 'big' return gifts. Amrita is looking for ways to make a simpler birthday party be as much fun for her child. It is difficult for her to demonstrate to her little kid that parties do not have to be about three-tier cakes and Barbie takeaways.

The over-the-top kiddie parties have spiralled out of all control. In the US, there is now 'Birthdays without Pressure', an informal citizen-action group that's trying to raise awareness and reverse the trend it calls 'out-of-control birthday parties'. The group came together in response to the increasingly lavish, competitive and unreal levels to which some parents had taken the simple kids' birthday party; the peer pressure and stress that this was causing, was something that the group decided needs to be tackled. They have come to a mutually agreed situation on a certain limit to spend in birthday parties and help each other to come up with innovative but not exotic ways for kids to have simple fun.

I'm sure it's not easy to get a five-year-old to see it that way, and her fascination with the big party and fancy take-home gifts is very understandable. However, it's important that we don't get caught up in trying to 'hard sell' anything to our kids. That smacks of insecurity and apologetic behaviour on our part, further reinforces in our kids a feeling of lack. It's best to just say that all parties don't have to be like that one and that you can have fun in your own way. While a child could be currently awed and taken up by what she experienced, by the time her birthday comes, you can start to plan her party with enthusiasm, and firmly but gently refuse to be drawn into comparisons with the other party.

For the long term, if you feel strongly about this, find like-minded parents who will think of interesting things to do on birthdays, instead of the big ostentatious party. This could include day trips out, simple, fun picnic food or kiddie cookouts, calling story tellers, renting fun films, etc. Don't feel apologetic about the cake not being three-tiered. Kids pick up vibes from you on such issues very sharply and if they feel that you are at ease with and enjoying throwing this party, that's what will remain in their minds ultimately, and not what you 'didn't provide'. By the time your child is eight or so, you could, like a lot of parents do, give them an either or option—a birthday party or a big gift. Usually kids choose the big gift, and the family can go out for a meal or make something special at home, or have a few friends come home for a night spend.

Without issuing homilies and guilt-inducing lectures, it is also important to subtly put some perspective on the table for our kids. You need to find ways to let them see how much they have on their birthday, compared to more than half the kids of the world or the kids around them. It may even be a good idea to include some kind, selfless acts on one's birthday, such as gifting new clothes or toys or books for a less privileged child or to an institution, and other such acts, where on a day you receive goodies and attention, you also give things and attention to someone else. Quite soon, you will be able to switch your child on to valuing and enjoying what she does have rather than focus on what she didn't get, on her birthday.

Most importantly, it is you who shouldn't get drawn into the trap of feeling as if you are un*able* to give the fairy tale party to your child.

Some parents battle this whole thing by trying to tell their children that parents who throw big parties are 'senseless'. Try and avoid this because it only teaches your child to deflect her genuine feelings. Sneering at the rich is as bad as sneering at the poor, and shouldn't be your line of action, however tempting that may be.

Dos and Don'ts

- Do not feel apologetic or defensive about not holding a big, ostentatious birthday bash for your kid. It may simply not be your priority.
- Birthdays can be a lot of fun without being lavish. Include trips, simple, fun picnic food or kiddie cookouts, calling story tellers, renting fun films, etc.
- Give your kid an option between a big gift or a birthday party. Most of them will take the big gift.
- Do not paint other parents who throw big parties for their children as 'bad' or 'senseless'.

Puberty

❧

Puberty is a trying and confusing time for children. Some young girls need to be helped to deal with the changes taking place in their bodies. How can we get our young girls to step into puberty with grace and self-love?

Mrs Sabnis's daughter is just a little over eleven, and is extremely embarrassed about her changing body shape as well as about having started her periods. Her mother has bought her trainer bras; the child has learnt to deal with the hygiene and such aspects of her periods too. However, she goes to great lengths not to let her father or younger brother even see her bras on the clothesline, does not let her mother refer to any of this in front of them, and when she gets her period she makes up all kinds of stories about why she won't go swimming, etc., to her close friends, anything to avoid bringing up the subject. She begs her mother to let her stay home from school, though she is not in pain, during that time.

Many young girls are mortified, as this child seems to be, at the onset of puberty and the early signs of womanhood.

It is a deep and perhaps unconscious discomfort with becoming and being now seen as a sexual being. And if she has begun to grow breasts before her classmates and other girls of her age, she could be particularly awkward on this count. Some girls are very pleased to develop, and will, also to their parents' bemusement, strut and talk about it all—the bra, the sanitary pads, all of that! Girls at both ends of this spectrum need to be taught to take their emerging feminity in their stride, and not make too much of it in either direction—not be embarrassed and hide, or not draw attention to it either. Perhaps this child also has a mistaken notion (kids jump to such conclusions, even if there is no mishandling of the situation by the parents) that she is in some way 'disgusting' to her father and brother. Her father must find some way to dismantle this embarrassment and the self-effacement that his daughter is trying to do.

Her mother would have to help this process, perhaps by telling the daughter that her father is a man of the world, knows about these things, and is proud and happy that his daughter is developing into a healthy, normal, young woman. Perhaps the mother can encourage, and her husband can actively think of, ways for the two of them to bond, in this new stage of her life. She must continue to feel precious and loved by her father. At this stage, it naturally happens that the physical contact between father and daughter reduces. While this is appropriate, he must keep a physical link with her, in a different form as it was when she was a little girl. This way, it will be easier for her to accept her changing and growing body in a self-loving, self-respecting way. Once this happens at home, it may be that she will be less likely to come up with elaborate stories and ploys to avoid mentioning simply that she has her periods.

As for staying home from school, perhaps her mother could indulge her on some days, and let her be at home, till she begins to take all of these bodily and emotional changes in her stride.

Dos and Don'ts

- The onset of puberty can prompt different reactions in young girls, sometimes intense embarrassment or the temptation to strut one's stuff. Both of them are extremities. Don't make too much fuss about the situation.
- Redefine the father–daughter relationship and work around the awkwardness, if any, by being very matter-of-fact about bodily changes and functions.

Public Behaviour

Having kids understand the difference between how they behave in public spaces and at home goes to making them more socially adjusted and pleasant to have around anywhere.

Nilanjan and Raksha have recently started taking their five and three-year-old kids to dine out with them at restaurants. Earlier it was just to open air or kiddy places. They tend to make a bit of noise and run around, even at 'grown-up' restaurants, which Raksha feels is okay. However, Nilanjan and Raksha totally differ on the way this has to be handled. He thinks there should be separate behaviour when in a public space like a restaurant. Basically he wants them to stay at the table and not raise their voices. Raksha feels it is fine if they run around a bit, as long as they don't annoy people. It depends really on what you perceive is 'annoying to other people'. Most restaurants in our country are bursting with kids running all over the place, getting in the way of the waiters, talking or crying very loudly, climbing on to the sofas with their footwear on and jumping, tapping on the fish tank, and suchlike! Most diners are a tolerant (long-suffering) lot, and loathe to yell at a kid, and so it appears that they don't mind.

But perhaps it's time we taught our kids that there is some distinction between private and public conduct. I know this may sound like some Victorian concept, but it isn't. When we adults go to dine out, we too dress appropriately, sit at our table, avoid talking and laughing or arguing very loudly (there are exceptions to this too!). These kinds of protocols exist all over the world, and not just at upscale restaurants and fancy clubs; it exists even in informal dining situations, and makes life easier for everyone. It doesn't mean that your kids have to be straight-jacketed and eat their dinner grimly silent. It just means that they modify their idea of fun, just like you do, in a public place. Most importantly, it means that they take into account the presence of other people.

Yes, kids need to remain at their table, and if there is something fascinating for them to look at, like a fish tank or a fountain or any kind of display in the restaurant, one of you could accompany them there to take a look, and get them to come back to the table without stopovers at other tables to peer at food and stare at people.

Dining out is also a family activity, and not, as a lot of people seem to think, a place where husband and wife can catch up with each other and the restaurant will take care of the kids and their entertainment. Parents can come up with ways to keep the kids engaged and involved at the table. It's a good way for the family to bond with each other, learn a few lessons in civic/public/considerate behaviour. You don't have to lecture them, you just need to communicate that they are not to behave as if they are at home, even if it is a 'family restaurant'. Kids should be gently 'pre-warned' before going out, about what they shouldn't do at a restaurant. Even very young people will soon get the point, and dining out (or going to any public space) will become more fun and doable.

Dos and Don'ts

- There is a difference between private and public spaces. Forewarn your kids about appropriate behaviour when you take them out for dining out, etc.
- There is a protocol that needs to be followed at a public place. Modify your kids' idea of fun and take into account the presence of other people.
- If there is something fascinating for the children to look at—fountain, fish tank etc, an adult could accompany them, rather than the kids being let loose.
- Keep it a family activity and engage your children. It is discourteous to do your own thing with your spouse, while leaving the restaurant staff to mind your boisterous kids.

Q for

⚜

Quick Fixes

Youngsters being 'wooed away' from higher studies and wrongly guided to earn a quick buck is a real problem. Parents need to find several allies in helping them guide their teenagers back on to the path.

Till the recession hit our shores, it was so tempting for many young people to dump their studies, and grab a job that gave them quick money like in BPOs or call centers, etc. Take the story of eighteen- year-old Malvika. A few months ago, she began to do part-time work for someone—a bit of writing, some spreadsheet tabulation, etc. Her parents were quite happy with this as she then told them they needn't give her any pocket money from now on. However, what ended up happening was, that she kept on taking more and more work, thus ignoring her studies. The money was good, and she began to re-think her goals—why bother to study beyond school if there was this kind of money to be made, she figured. She could pick up various skills on the job, instead of a boring classroom, was her logic. The freelancer she was doing the work for, also influenced her heavily to not bother with further studies.

That's an unfortunate and immature conclusion that Malvika drew. It looks like the person influencing her was pretty short-sighted as well as unscrupulous too. Her parents tried to reason with their daughter, but the immediate gains—the flush of money, and the feeling that annoying and difficult studies are not needed at all –blinded her thoroughly.

In such situations, parents need to enlist the help of other adults, preferably young adults who're earning as well as have qualified and got good jobs as a result of their qualifications. Someone of that profile will be able to tell Malvika more convincingly, that there is more to a working life than earning money. There's mental challenge, there's growth, there's exposure to the larger world, all waiting for her if she goes beyond the lure of money right now. This person who you find to speak to your youngster, should explain that she will remain a 'coolie' labour if she decides to be satisfied with the bucks that are coming her way easily, and does not qualify for anything better. Also, our impressionable children must be guided to know that entire industries change or vanish, and it is essential to acquire many different skill sets.

Dos and Don'ts

- ✇ Enlist the help of young adults who are earning well after being professionally qualified.
- ✇ Help her understand that working life is more than just about making money and there is a whole world out there waiting for her to explore.
- ✇ Any industry can bust these days and it is important that she acquires other skill-sets.

R for

Relocation

Stay in the background, when helping your child finding acceptance and new friends if you move to a new town or city. Intervene only if things get really hard for your child.

Mita and Gautam have moved recently from another city. Their daughter Shakya is seven. In the complex where they now live, the other kids are just not ready to include her in the group. The children complain that she talks loudly and rudely if things don't go her way in a game. Mita feels that all children behave this way sometime or the other, so this is just a way the other kids have of picking on her child. Many times, they run away and hide when she goes down to play and she comes back crying almost every day. Things are not like this at school, where Shakya is happy. Mita as well as Gautam tried to talk to some of the children in their complex, who are all a little older than her, but that made it worse, because they began calling her 'complaint box'. Mita is now worried about where all this is headed, and whether her child is now 'sentenced' to be friendless. She is toying with the idea of speaking to the other parents but fears that this may isolate Shakya even more.

Things do get a little difficult, even brutal, at the playground sometimes. And once a child is targeted, the herd mentality could take over, and everyone begins to pick on that particular child which becomes a rather distressful time for parents and the child. Mita and Gautam have done the important thing of listening to their child's distress, trying to understand the dynamics between her and the other kids, and intervening in some way. However, while they have tried to intervene in good faith, perhaps now is the time to step back and not run to the child's help. This is difficult, but the cycle of her complaining and you trying to sort out matters for her needs to be now broken. Being picked on is bad enough, and then being labeled a cry-baby makes it much worse and difficult to sort out. In a situation like this, parents could start by saying that for one week, the child is not to come and tell you anything, but just handle it in whatever way she wants.

In the meanwhile, you must find ways to help your child at home with the socializing process. For instance, you could teach him or her how to be assertive and not necessarily aggressive when she wants to lead in a game or put her point across about anything. This is an important distinction. This would also involve teaching her that rudeness gets you nowhere.

A child in this situation could also redirect herself to some other activities, where she may find more acceptance amongst her peer group at such places, so that her social life is not dependent on the housing complex children. Moreover, all of this may blow over, once she has been there long enough for the building kids to accept her.

Talking to other parents is not such a good idea. They tend to be defensive, and the whole issue gets dragged into the adult realm of blame. If you think there are a few parents out there with the maturity to see it as your asking for help for your child, rather than complaining about their child, then you could venture to involve them.

Dos and Don'ts

- If you can help it, do not interfere with the child's problem for a week and let her think things over.
- Meanwhile help her with the socializing process at home, wherein she can be guided to be assertive about a point without being loud and aggressive.
- Redirect her to other activities where she might find more peer acceptance. That way she does not have to rely entirely on kids in your complex.
- Such problems tend to tide over sooner or later.

Rudeness

When an adolescent uses cheeky or downright rude responses to communicate with you, there are several strategies that a parent can adopt, to 'dismantle' this kind of behaviour, without escalating the battle.

Shubhra's 14 year old daughter is at times subtly rude to her parents and even to her grandparents. Either it is back-chat, or eye-rolling or muttering 'whatever', etc. She gives Shubhra a cutting or stand-offish or ridiculing reply to something simple that she asks, when a simple yes, or no, or okay would have done fine. Shubhra ends up feeling hurt and ridiculed.

Back-chat and eye-rolling etc. are shocking to encounter in your kids. Especially when you are at the receiving end. Part of it comes naturally as a form of rebellion and of asserting their own 'grown-up' right to respond with sarcasm; but part of it is learnt, and comes from watching TV teenagers doing their rude things. While you can let some of it slide, and not jump on every instance and upbraid your kids, don't let them get away with it too often.

One, that you sometimes shut down on her when she behaves in this way. Simply close down the communication, leave the room, and do something else. For all that hard-nosed cynicism that they display, your silence is something most kids can't take.

The other option is to talk with your child, explaining that you feel hurt (however, remember not to whine and plead with her) with her behaviour, and explain clearly to her that some of the things she's biting your head off for are just social and family niceties. Tell her that you can all totally stop saying them to her, if she is incapable of receiving them in the way they are meant. For instance, one teenager always came up with snappy-nasty replies if she was asked nurturing questions like 'Did you sleep well?' or 'Ready for dinner?' The replies would be on the lines of: "No, I'm a raging insomniac' or 'Do I have a choice?' and other such stuff. Her parents decided, and told her, that till she 'understood' such conversations and their emotional content, they wouldn't talk in a nurturing way to her at all.

Remember that there is also a certain enjoyment that teenagers derive out of using language in an effective (albeit nasty) fashion. Sarcasm, believe it or not, reflects a child's growing mental capabilities! Seriously. Making snide comments lets them feel smart and grown-up. No doubt, however, that it's no fun being at the receiving end of their target practise.

Some people find it just infinitely easier to put up with the back-chat and expect grandparents and other adults at the receiving end to put up with it too. That's not a good idea. It's best to understand where they're coming from, when they use snubbing, sneering language, but use a range of responses to get them to tone it down and stop it.

Dos and Don'ts

- One, that you sometimes shut down on her when she behaves in this way. Simply close down the communication, leave the room, and do something else. For all that hard-nosed cynicism that they display, your silence is something most kids can't take.

- The other thing to do is to laughingly say: "oh you're in that kind of mood". This way you communicate that it is some strange impulse or motive on your child's part, and not 'dumb' behaviour on your part that prompts him or her to behave this way. Make her rude talk and expressions sound like silly behaviour, and she may come off it. Warning: she may get even more incensed for a while, but may ultimately stop it.

- Sometimes laugh with your child, and say something like: "ok, that was smart and funny, but it was incredibly rude". And after this, expect a reply to your original question or an apology (on a good day). You may find that this strategy works best, because it acknowledges the word-play, but rejects the rude sentiment attached to it.

S for

Sex Education

Some parents take the 'ostrich' attitude while some parents agonize over how to have 'the talk' with their kids. Talking about the body, sex, porn, is something that is a must.

The Mukund family is conflicted about sex education for their kids, an eleven-year-old boy and twelve-year-old girl. The father feels that there is no need to get into a conversation, and that he himeself got 'educated' by default and this has worked fine for him - his parents never had any chat with him on this. He even feels that having a formal chat increases curiosity unnecessarily? Children these days already seem to know quite a lot anyway, is his other argument. Mrs Mukund feels that, in line with current trends, they simply must sit down as a family, and have The Talk, but she just doesn't see how she's going to do this, without support from her husband.

There are many different ages and stages at which you talk to your kids about sex. There is no single 'the-birds-and-the-bees talk' which one can have and 'get it over with'. As Mr Mukund says, kids today have already got some ideas and inputs on the subject. However, those are often sketchy, out and out wrong, or surrounded by much speculation, giggling and a kind of lurid interest! What you can do at various stages of your child's growing up is to provide age-appropriate information on sex—both the physical aspects and the emotional ones. Parents' role in this matter, most importantly, is to provide healthy non-awkward information and dismantle the wrong notions, guilt, and the kind of 'ikky fascination' that kids have about the subject.

I don't believe that being educated by default is a good idea. Sure, some people grew up stumbling upon information and dealing with their own sexual desires and encounters in whatever way they could. However, why avoid and side-step an issue and risk your child getting warped ideas and being drawn into experimentation, porn, etc. without having armed him in any way with any knowledge or emotional preparedness on the subject?

It's important for a parent too to be at ease with the subject, and also know how much he/she would like to discuss. There are many books in the market, especially to show your child diagrams and functions of sexual and reproductive organs. However, the emotional and social implications of sex and sexual behaviour, etc. must come from you. I suggest parents avoid bringing in religion, God, punishment, permission, etc., and keep the conversation about sex as an extension of a respectful, joyous and loving relationship with a partner.

As for porn, it exists out there and what you can hope to do is restrict access on the internet. Avoid labelling it too heavily as 'evil' and 'disgusting' etc. Perhaps you can, over time, stress that sex is a one-to-one interaction that can be healthy and fulfilling.

You could definitely ask your child's school to introduce sex education at various levels. There are many excellent sex educators who could conduct sessions in schools. In such sessions, children are also encouraged to write anonymous questions, which are read out and adequately answered. Of course, this does not mean that parents avoid talking about sex with their kids. It just means that, in addition to parents, other responsible adults provide information and help kids deal with their emerging sexuality.

Dos and Don'ts

- ❧ Since most parents don't broach the topic of sex at all, many teenagers just end up stumbling upon the information and dealing with their own sexual desires and encounters in whatever way they can. But this may not be the best approach. Why allow them to get warped ideas and being drawn into experimentation, porn, etc? Do not side-step talk on sex.

- ❧ Your role as a parent is to provide age-appropriate information to your children, where you remove feelings of guilt and disgust and also dismantle any wrong notions they may have about sex.

- ❧ Ask your child's school to introduce sex education at various levels.

Smacking

Spare the rod, yes, but some parents find that the longer route of time-outs, cutting off privileges, and other such punishments is sometimes the more painful and traumatizing route.

Jyoti used to slap her child till he was seven—a light smack on the bottom or on the shoulder at times. Some of her friends found this really shocking and she had to find other ways of getting him to note her displeasure about something that he had said or done. Jyoti tried the time-out method, explaining patiently what the child had done was wrong, and even taking away some privileges like not letting him use the computer for two days, or no playing outside for some time, etc. Jyoti and other parents like her found the other methods of punishment much more stressful for both of them as well as the child. A smack registers then and there and that's it. The other methods amount to a lot of whining, which is exhausting for them.

The degree of hurt (physical and emotional) that comes with the smack/slap can be debated—most kids are okay with a little smack, which causes no bodily harm, but it should definitely never be done in front of other people. Why smacking is becoming increasingly a no-no, starting from the Western world, is because there is a very thin line between the kind of smack that Jyoti is talking about and 'beatings', accompanied by verbal abuse and shouting, etc. A frustrated and angry parent can cross the line easily, which is what many parents found about themselves, and perhaps that is why there is such a growing informal ban on smacking kids. Equally, the taking away of privileges or the time-out, go-to-your-room stuff also can be pretty traumatic for any child (and the parent) as the child will keep fuming, crying, sulking and trying to negotiate or argue, sometimes for days on end, if the punishment involves three days of no computer games or other such embargos.

The mother of a five-year-old says that she prefers to take the longer route of explaining and communicating to her daughter why certain behaviour is upsetting to the mother or socially and emotionally wrong. She feels that she has got some success this way, rather than getting things done out of the child's fear of the slap/smack.

Many parents say that reaching out and smacking a child or shouting at him/her occurs when they feel that there is some immediate danger to the child or to someone else around the child because of his behaviour, when something needs to be done right then to stop the behaviour. Others feel the urge to smack their child when something has been explained many times to a child—why he or she shouldn't do something—and the child still keeps on doing it.

Earlier generations were quite unapologetic to use a smack, and even today there are some parents who will come right out and say it can be used to great effect without any major trauma to the child. However, it is equally true that it does teach kids to 'talk with their hands' when they come up against something that they can't deal with themselves. Here, too, opinion is sharply divided; there are some who believe that slapping or hitting a child fosters aggression and some who believe that it shows the child that there are sometimes physical consequences of terrible behaviour, and this helps the child put a lid on its own aggression.

However, it's a tough call. I know parents who never smack but who traumatize their kids in many other ways. And I would say that while smacking a kid is looked upon with such outrage by some, not enough attention is paid to how verbally abusive a parent or teacher can be, and that too without using any 'bad words', but by saying extremely harsh, dismissive, and demeaning things to the child.

I think the thumb rule or measure of any punishment should be about the residual trauma to both child and parent. So when it comes to the smack, if both of you can move on—you not covered in guilt and the child not in a cloud of resentment and hurt—then perhaps it is okay to do so when things get out of hand.

Dos and Don'ts

- ❧ Both smacking and taking away privileges are scenarios that come with their share of issues. Judge the situation and tread carefully.
- ❧ Be aware that sometimes verbal abuse is far more traumatizing to a child than a smack.
- ❧ Play it by the ear and choose a punishment that is least damaging to both you and your child.

Socialization

Having kids attend family functions and be sociable is important, but not easy to do if they see absolutely no reason or interest in the event. It has got to be part of a larger process of involvement with family, and not just something that parents insist on at festival times.

The Mathan kids, aged thirteen and fifteen, have become very difficult to deal with during the festival time in the last couple of years, and it is getting worse every year. They have both declared that they do not like anything about the celebrations—the sweets or the savoury dishes, crackers, festive clothes, and they just do not like going to visit relatives. The parents have to coax them out of their rooms when people visit. Mrs Mathan is willing to let them be, but her husband feels that this is just snobbery on their part and that they must learn to enter the spirit of the season. This is the same when it comes to attending weddings. The parents don't want them participating as if they're doing the whole world a favour, and they don't want to let them opt out of all social occasions as well.

However, how does one get an adolescent and a teenager to be more sociable? The snobbery part may be true, but they may also be extremely bored with these activities. The 'spirit of the season' does not necessarily mean enjoying all the things that you have outlined for your children because they may not enjoy what you do. Perhaps you could try to break these things down into necessary and unnecessary activities, and literally negotiate what they can skip and what must be done. If it is the 'snobbery' that hassles you, then there is a larger issue, that of being better connected to the family and friends network, to be tackled year-round really. If, for you, visiting relatives or at least being sociable and nice to people when they visit is important, then you need to have a sensitive chat with them about why they need to connect with people better—not just as a favour to you.

If you are only visiting your relatives during the festive season and have no connection with them otherwise, your forcing or coaxing your children to meet them now will seem artificial and difficult to enjoy. It makes sense to, pre-season, perhaps clue them on who's who in the larger family, and tell them a little something about your own relationship with that person and why you like and respect him/her. All of this means that we can't simply uncork 'the festive season' on our kids. We need them to have some small connection in whatever little way with who their family is and why they are important. Of course, many kids this age are preoccupied with themselves, and don't have the mental space or don't get what the big fuss about festivals and weddings is.

Whichever part of the festivities are really important

to you, you need to negotiate with them, talking about the things/activities they have to do and other things they could learn to enjoy or participate in. There could be a list of things that you could agree to let go off so that they are not constantly reluctant participants.

Dos and Don'ts

- Make sure that your children are connected with other family members or friends who are important to you, so that they don't feel like they are meeting people who are complete strangers.
- Tell your children something interesting or an anecdote about so and so member in the family. It will make them keener to be part of the event.
- Negotiate with your teenagers on events that are important to you and insist that they attend. But give them leeway on other occasions.

Stealing

Teaching kids not to steal or that stealing is wrong involves age-appropriate lessons about boundaries, honesty, and owning up.

Ten-year-old Aman sometimes pinches money from his mother's purse or from the change kept in a small drawer in the kitchen. When confronted, he either says he didn't take it, or laughs it off saying, 'Just for fun' or, 'You would have given it to me anyway because i wanted to buy paper' etc. Should parents just ignore this, or take it seriously? This is a tight-rope walk for any parent. Does one laugh it off with just a 'you bad boy' kind of tiny admonition, or does one read the child the riot-act? Parents tend to fall on either side of the rope! It's easy to laugh it off for some parents, and for some, it is also easy to give vent to fears and pet-theories, and turn it into a full-blown family crisis, in which the parents punish, lecture, and 'awfulize' the situation by concluding grimly that the child is showing signs of becoming devious and will grow up to become a criminal.

The more complex and demanding requirement from a parent is to come up with an appropriate response. Which would be:

a) to communicate their disapproval without rejecting and labelling the child outright

b) to talk about, in age-appropriate terms, the concept of boundaries, both physical and abstract, which means that sneaking into his mother's bag as well as taking stuff that is not his, is a no-no.

As for the explanation that, 'You would have given it to me anyway'—this must be turned right round, by saying 'Well, in that case, why not ask me, and not do it behind my back'? This applies to money as well as his parents' things. Our kids must feel that their parents are there for them as providers and nurturers, and that their parents are happy to give them the things that they need and enjoy. But when children take it for granted, and simply grab or pinch things, they need to be pulled off the road for a quiet talk that brings in important concepts like boundaries, rules, and honesty.

Another level at which parents can take the conversation is to talk about how the world around the child largely functions well for him because of the honesty of people around him. He can be given a few scenarios in the 'What if' format. What if the domestic help took something of yours without asking, assuming you were going to give it to her anyway? What if your school simply took money from our bank without asking, saying you were going to pay us anyway? What if one of your friends stole a toy or game from you which you would have readily given him if he had asked? Parents should remember to undertake these conversations in a loving and 'us' mode—implying that even the grown-ups around him whom he loves and respects, work hard at being fair and honest. Also get to another core issue, as gently as is possible, about whether he feels awkward to ask for things. The conversation would help him learn to simply ask, whether they are things that his parents would easily give him, or things that they would need to think about before giving him.

Dos and Don'ts

- ❧ Show disapproval but do not label or condemn the kid.
- ❧ Make your child feel that you are there for them as providers and to take care of his needs and wants. But boundaries are something to be respected.
- ❧ A good technique is to put him through the 'what if' scenario. What if your friend took your toys without asking? This will immediately strike a chord with your kid.

Stepchildren

A new, changed equation in the family means that children need to be given time and space to accept the new step-parent and build bridges at their own pace.

Tarak is soon to become the step-father of six-year-old Omkar. His parents divorced two years ago. The child meets his birth father once a week. While Tarak does get along with the child, and the child is fond of Tarak too, both are not comfortable with the mother insisting that Omkar begin to call his step father Papa (he calls his father Daddy). He began by calling Tarak Uncle, and they feel it's fine to stick to that.

Firstly, 'making' a child call the new 'parent' anything is a bad idea. It is understandable that perhaps Omkar's mother is anxious that the three of them become a family as quickly as possible. But this cannot be done by force-fitting relationships in place. So its much better to let mutual trust, love and acceptance slowly fall into place, by actions rather than the enforced label of 'Papa'. All that the insistence will do is cause the child to be uncomfortable and confused, which can quickly spiral into being resentful and angry over the new step father's presence. This is a complex time for the child, especially since he is in regular touch with his biological father. Accepting his exit, and the presence of a new man in his mother's life cannot be easy, not for a 6 year old—and usually not for anyone. Seeing one parent as a 'couple' with someone new is quite an emotionally demanding experience for a child which is not to say that it is wrong, or shouldn't happen, of course. It's just that the situation simply has to be handled sensitively and with the faith that things will fall into place in their own time.

Dos and Don'ts

- Tarak has obviously started out on the right foot, if both he and the child like each other. It's important that Tarak make it very clear to the child that he is free to call him whatever he likes.
- What is important too is to allay the mother's anxieties and convince her not to insist on this name-switch.

Studying Abroad

With many parents opting to send undergraduate kids off to Western universities for all-expenses-paid educations, it has become something of an urban trend. Parents who cannot afford it or do not feel the need to send kids abroad at such a high cost, are hard-pressed to put their point across to their kids.

Most of the kids in Prakash's child's 10th standard class (she goes to a premium school which offers excellent education) are headed straight to all-expenses-paid-by-parents undergrad education in countries like the US, Australia, Singapore or the EU after they finish school. Both his wife and he don't believe in this kind of a thing at all. The parents and their kids who are being sent talk despairingly about the poor standard of higher education here, which is true to some extent. But neither can Prakash afford to send his children without scholarships nor does he and his wife think things are so bad here. Moreover, they don't want to send them off so young. However, the problem is that their older daughter is beginning to feel bad and at times upset about the fact that she is not part of the 'club' that already talks about SAT scores and 'statement of purpose' essays, and names of foreign universities, and the likes.

It's a tricky balance for parents in Prakash's situation, to not dismiss the other kids around her as 'spoilt', and yet highlight to their daughter the merits of being on-the-ground here in India. Firstly, you have to be totally unapologetic about not affording to send her off abroad. There are many things that we simply had to lump about what our parents could or could not do for us, or would or would not do for us. We may have not liked it then and felt most sorry for ourselves, as grown ups we can now see the wisdom of our parents' choices. This could well be one of those things for your daughter.

However, right now you don't want to simply tell her to 'deal with it' of course. What you can do is emphasize that a hard-won scholarship is something worth waiting and working for. This may sound to her like some old-fashioned insistence on your part, but so be it.

The other thing a parent could do is get the son or daugther to meet slightly older youngsters who have opted for courses in India and are happy with the education they are getting. You and your child should research on the Internet and through other sources, what her options are, so that she doesn't see her future as some 'choose from the best of a bad lot' kind of scenario. Currently, with everyone around Prakash's daughter flapping their wings (and their parents flexing their wallet muscles), she is beginning to feel left behind, even before she embarks on anything. It is this that you have to tackle sensitively and yet decisively. Avoid getting defensive with your child in this situation which means don't say things like 'I'm sorry this is all we can afford.' Don't go on the offensive either, with statements like 'What's wrong with our country, we have a glorious tradition of education,' etc! Simply be secure and comfortable in the knowledge that you will do what you can for your kids.

Dos and Don'ts

- When we work hard for our kids and they make us feel like we are not 'measuring up', it is very tempting to say something bitter and scathing to get them to appreciate your position. Do avoid this at all costs. Your child is in a way a victim of the peer pressure around him or her.
- Send out an unapologetic, yet understanding signal to your youngster about what you will and will not do for him or her on this count.

Swearing

When boys get fascinated with using bad words, dads must come into the picture and make their sons see that swearing is silly, and certainly not macho.

Nine-year-old Ronit's parents are worried. He has been picking up some slang as well as abusive language from his companions in school and on the school bus. No adult or teenagers in the house or extended family or neighbourhood use such words and the family is aghast seeing the words he has begun to use. He often does not know what the words mean, and merely has a warped explanation from some friend. Some words the parents have been able to explain and tell him why they are offensive. But there are some that simply cannot be explained to him but it is important that he stop using them.

It is awkward and unnecessary to explain the actual meaning of some crude words and phrases, and it is quite impossible to do that for every such word that a child picks up. However, he can be told very firmly that you will not allow that kind of language in the family. Sometimes boys need to hear some wise words and some rules about swearing from their fathers—and to learn from their father that it is just stupid and not macho or hip to talk in this way. Stereotypically, moms are seen as softies and not 'one of the guys' in the swearing fun. 'Everyone's mom doesn't like swearing, big deal,' is the attitude. However, if dad comes into the picture, and clearly disapproves, or better still dismisses swearing and cussing as silly behaviour, and shows zero tolerance towards it, that may have a much better impact.

When adults explain the meaning of any of the abusive words to a child, it is more important to explain the 'emotional charge' or the weightage of that word when it is used - especially if the words are racist/communal or sexist or hurtful to people with disabilities.

Often a few disliked teachers or timid or overweight kids are the target of a lot of this kind of school bus swearing and name-calling. A parent could bring this up in the school's PTA and try to also get the school to address this issue about language used in the school bus too.

However, keep in mind that parents also need to use a big dose of the 'ignore vaccine' at home. Try to be matter of fact and not encourage children to think it is either funny or specially interesting and striking, when they swear and cuss. You could just say firmly "We don't use that word and I don't want to hear it again." Next time he uses it, ignore him and become unavailable to him for a while—emotionally, verbally, physically.

In some families, one parent or relative swears and - this gives mixed messages to kids. Most adults try to keep their own swearing in check around kids, but it comes out at times. However, you can again clearly say 'that is his problem' if your kids ever say, 'But uncle Ramesh uses the eff-word'.

If your son uses a swear word when he is angry about something or someone, you could encourage him to say what he really feels. Let the word he used go, but insist on knowing what he is so angry about. This way, you again get him to see that swearing is not a sign of being smart, it is more a sign that the person who swears simply doesn't know a better word to use. You could also allow him to come up with a few 'permissible' words to use when he's upset about something. One mother has got her 12-year-old to stop using what she had labelled 'rude words'. Now, once in a while, he comes up with something like: 'All people who honk loudly on the road are real…real…rude words'!

Dos and Don'ts

- ❧ It's best if the dad comes into the picture, and clearly disapproves, or better still dismisses swearing and cussing as silly behaviour, and shows zero tolerance for it. It will show the kid that swearing is not macho.
- ❧ When you explain the meaning of any of the abusive words to a child, it is more important to explain the 'emotional charge' or the weightage of that word when it is used - especially if the words are racist/communal or sexist or hurtful to people with disabilities.
- ❧ Ignore the swear word used sometimes and insist on knowing what is making your child so angry. This way he understands that swearing is not smart and is used by those who simply do not know a better word.

T for

Taste

❧

We have to let our kids develop and exercise their own taste, which may end sometimes in some rather odd clothing and other choices, but that is part of the growing up process.

Vandita, almost six, has started insisting on choosing her own clothes to wear in the morning to go to school (they do not have a uniform). Her grandmom as well as her dad, both think that this is a good thing. While her mother agrees, she finds that she either wears the same three sets of clothes in rotation, ignoring the rest, or pairs oddly matched clothes. If she tells her it is looking silly or suggests something else, Vandita throws a big tantrum about it, stressing on the fact that her mom doesn't let her do anything at all. In addition, the older daughter, eleven-year-old Sasha, wants to choose things like curtains and cushions and knick-knacks, etc. for the house, and her taste is very different from that of her parents. But they do want to let them exercise their choices in such things to some extent, or how else would they develop their own taste and choice?

Perhaps it would be best to let the younger one, who is

throwing together her own clothes, and seems currently very touchy about any suggestions from her mom, just do whatever she likes. If she's wearing odd combinations, her feedback will come from her friends, maybe even in a slightly cruel mocking form. Ideally, we don't want our kids to be pointed or mocked at, but part of developing a sense of what one wears comes from the outside world, and partly from our parents. Vandita is at the age where asserting her autonomy differently from her mom is important in small things like what she chooses to wear, and it is best that her parents grin and bear it when it comes to her choice of clothes. Sometimes if you don't comment at all, you may well find that your children will come to you and ask you how they look. At that time you could choose to simply say 'nice', if you think that she is still in a state where she will react strongly to anything that you say. If there is room for you to give genuine feedback, your response should not involve words like 'silly' or 'mismatched'. Word your reply in a more positive wat—'This dress looks nicer with your green tights', or 'I liked that skirt better when you wore it with the short t-shirt.'

As for letting kids get involved in selecting things for home décor, many parents encourage it, but restrict it to the child's own room and things. But do take into account her taste or likings for some of the smaller things around the house, even if you don't necessarily like it. It's part of the family dynamics to arrive at something that one person may really like, while the others are lukewarm about. Do make it a point not to be apologetic or mocking about something in your house to visitors; sometimes we are anxious for people to know that some things (not to your taste) were not chosen by you! When you do that, it defeats the purpose of letting your kids exercise and develop their own taste and opinions. Do ask her opinion on some things, even if you have bought them on your own. Give your kids room to express aesthetic values, not just to things that are bought and brought into the house, but to the world around them.

Dos and Don'ts

- Grin and bear your child's insistence on choosing their own clothes. Kids want to exert their autonomy by that age.
- Let the feedback for their clothes, jewellery, décor, etc., come from their friends.
- Give them suggestions on what might look better when they are in a less defensive mood.
- Take your children's ideas about home decor, but restrict it mostly to their own room. When it comes to smaller things, be more willing to accept their tastes even if it doesn't match with yours.

Teasing

❧

Parents have to intervene very carefully for a child who is a victim of constant teasing. A combination of teaching your child to handle the teasing as well as getting the teasers to get rid of their meanness, is what the strategy would need to be.

Parul's nine-year-old son is constantly getting teased at school. His clothes and look are always the butt end of jokes (even though there's nothing different there), and it hurts him a lot to be called a 'pansy' and other such offensive terms because he's not the sporty sort. Parul wants to step in and complain to the principal. Her husband says no, because there's been no physical violence, and that it's important that he learn to defend himself. What should the solution be for parents who have a child that is being bullied?

I think that it is important that they learn to take some of this stuff on the chin, ignore it, or even give back, measure for measure. Before stepping in (which you may have to do if it gets relentless or physical), a parent can help their kids in this situation with a few strategies.

Firstly, ignoring the teasing. This you can do by painting

the teasers in a 'boring' light in conversations at home. Like they're a stuck record. Right now they're his tormentors but if he sees them as silly fellows with nothing better to do, he may be able to ignore them better.

The second strategy is teasing right back. A few smart come-backs, which involves targeting some trait of the teaser may go a long way in getting the bullies to back off. While this is not something one likes to do, you might have to help him actually find something to laugh at about them, and thus go prepared with a little 'verbal ammo'! Try to get him to do this in a kidding off-hand manner, and not cruelly.

Another way to frustrate teasers is to agree with whatever he says in a bland or funny way. You could get your child to say things like 'Of course my shirt is funny, so what?' or 'Ya I wore this just so that you could laugh; see how kind I am.'

About the name-calling, particularly 'pansy' and suchlike, parents might just need to step in at some point, and do three things:

- Get the teacher in charge or principal to have a talk about this to the class/school in general, particularly on the issue of studious students versus sports lovers, and the pointlessness of the so-called 'divide'.
- Take the intervention a step forward by calling up the teaser's parents and having a (hopefully) calm conversation about this.
- Casually dropping in at the end of a school day and addressing some light warning or just a friendly appeal

to the teasers themselves to put an end to it. This should preferably be done by both parents, because with boys, 'your mama came to save you' kind of teasing can quickly follow if only the mother is seen to be protecting her son. Both parents standing firmly behind the bullied child sends out a better signal.

While all this sounds like the stuff of strategic war manoeuvers, do try to carry them out as casually as possible, so that your teased child can put all this in perspective and it doesn't turn into an unsavoury episode in his life.

Dos and Don'ts

- Ignore the tormentors and treat them as 'boring' topics in dinner conversations at home.
- Let your child come up with a sharp repartee that will put the teasing kid in his place.
- If the teasing gets too personal, consult the principal or school teacher on what can be done.
- Casually drop into the class and make a mild but firm warning to the teasers so that they get the point.

Tomboy

There are vulnerabilities and anxieties hiding behind the tough exterior of a 'tomboy'. She needs to be helped to accept and be comfortable with her femininity.

Tomboy. It is a word many consider a passé today, but one that is easily identifiable –. Garima's fourteen-year-old daughter Tanvi is a tomboy. She is pretty with fine features, but she stays unkempt and dresses and walks about like a boy. She bullies other girls, and even the boys are a bit afraid of her. In reality, she means no harm and is not a malicious or mean child. She just seems to want to be tough and use rough humour. For instance, her teacher reported that she recently bullied a boy by sitting on his journal and then giving it back to him and saying, 'I farted on your journal'. While everyone enjoys this kind of joking in her class, her parents and her teachers think that she should become a little more lady-like!

Often one of the two (or both) factors operate when a girl goes the 'tomboy' way. Firstly, with some girls it is a way of not coming to terms with ones growing body and femininity and male interest in them. Secondly, with some girls it comes (perhaps unconsciously) from another factor—the 'female role' ascribed by the society around us that she is rejecting with her actions and her boy-like attitude. Perhaps girls like Tanvi live in a city or town or community environment where the implicit and explicit messages are that girls are weak or 'lesser' than men; girls have to ultimately be groomed only to be good wives and mothers; a young girl is fair game for sexual harassment ranging from 'eve-teasing' to more aggressive forms; girls have to play coy-shy games to be attractive to boys and other such overt and covert messages. Another factor that sometimes operates is an overload of aggression in the child, and this finds its way to the surface most easily by 'male' behaviour.

While I would urge parents who have a tomboy in their family not to make a big deal about this (because it ends up making her feel that she has to live up to a reputation more and more), perhaps there are a few things that you as well as any sensitive teacher willing to collaborate with you could do. Firstly, help her to find ways in accepting her emerging feminine body. You can take her shopping and point out more feminine clothes that need not necessarily be frilly and girlie, but are less manly versions of what she's already wearing. For instance, better fitting jeans for women, shirts but ones cut to her body shape. This can be done without discussion, by just pointing her to such choices and telling her how nice she looks in them.

Equally, it's important not to make a big deal when she does something more 'girlish' or dresses femininely on your insistence (say for a wedding or any other such occasion). People feel that they must gush and re-inforce how wonderful the feminine behaviour or look is and how it suits her. This only scares tomboys into rushing back into their comfort zone.

A father's role in this stage of such a girl's life is important. Do see that he maintains a close relationship with her, and does not admonish her 'to act more like a woman'. A father should acknowledge his tomboy's femininity in subtle ways. Both the parents as well as her teacher can encourage and reward (and notice, firstly) some of the small sensitive things that she does, and help her to feel that being loud and raucous is not her only identity.

Do help her to also see that there are many ways that one can be (and there are plenty of role models of this around really) a woman and yet in control of one's life, choices, and environment.

The other thing is to address her aggression, if there is a lot of it present in her, and find a way to have her express and deal with it, rather than assume ruffian postures. There are vulnerabilities and anxieties hiding behind that demeanour, and if you draw these out and tackle them, you will have done your 'tomboy' a service.

Dos and Don'ts

- Help the girl choose clothes that are more feminine. Not the frilly kinds, but perhaps less manly ones.
- All the same do not excessively compliment her when she wears something feminine. That scares tomboys.
- The father could appreciate some aspects of her femininity, without criticizing her for being tomboyish.

U for

Unfairness

Teaching children to deal with unfairness and insensitivity from the adult world, especially from teachers and other 'guru' figures, is possibly one of the most complex and unpleasant demands of parenting.

Rajini and Hemant's seven-year-old daughter Sia is a friendly, sensitive child. She loves all forms of dancing and is good at it. She does not understand why her dance teacher in school does not select her to participate in competitions and school functions. She points at a couple of kids who are regularly selected for these events, wondering what is lacking in her. When the parents enquired at school they came to know that the dance teacher favours those kids who take private tuitions from her. How do parents get a little child to accept the concept of partiality or bias and that it is a part of life?

We all wish that our children didn't have to learn such lessons about discriminatory people and situations in the world so young. However, we have to teach our children to take this in their stride. In such a situation, you could consider sending her to another dance class, quite different and more evolved than the one she attends. If your child is ever in a situation like the one I mentioned look for a sensitive nice soul who teaches dance, which I'm sure will not be difficult to get. This way at least our kids don't come to the conclusion that the unfairness they may face from one person translates immediately and decisively to absence of opportunities everywhere.

Even more important, and tricky, is to help our kids take away focus from being 'selected' by such people, and to simply enjoy the dance or any such activity for itself. This is no doubt easier said than done, given the atmosphere of 'excelling' and 'performing' and 'picking up prizes' in today's world. All kids quite naturally want so much for their teachers to like and appreciate them.

When dealing with this kind of a situation, you have to find a fine balance, hit the right note, without actually scoffing openly at the teacher or spelling out to your child that the teacher and her opinions and decisions don't mean anything in the larger picture of things. You have to convey this to your child, subtly. On the other hand, it won't do (and is not easy either) to tell our kids in such situations to take a lofty, detached stand, and to continue pursuing their hobby without expecting positive strokes from their teacher. Some parents, in their bid to shield their kids from the hurtful reality of being overlooked by someone like this dance teacher, go out of their way to try and get a child to take an abstract view of things, with elaborate advice and information about dealing with prejudice, such as: 'Just close your eyes, and keep doing your own thing, don't look for the fruits and rewards', and other such quasi-philosophical things, that don't cut much ice with a child. It would be much better to: a) just acknowledge that the teacher seems to be unfair and biased and; b) find other more sensitive people for pursuits like this.

It's also important not to become a victim yourself as well as your child, with cynical statements like: 'It's a cruel harsh world out there' or 'true talent is rarely recognized, it's only pushy people who get ahead.'

So the balance then is to get your kid to not take the teachers' opinions and actions by the word, but first to assess their own interests seriously. Even though this is difficult for most adults to do in their own lives and is even more intricate when you're imparting this as a parent, it is still worth the effort, as you will be enabling your child to look and grow past people and situations like this.

Dos and Don'ts

- If you are convinced that your child is bearing the brunt of an unjust teacher, and her talent and morale are suffering, it's best you look for a more sensitive teacher.
- Lofty ideas that unfairness exists in the world does not cut ice with kids. Acknowledge the problem and work towards finding a solution. Your child's interests need not suffer for a teacher's opinion.

V for

Valuing

It does children a lot of good to learn to value what mom and dad do, especially when stay-at-home moms get back to working. Enjoy and respect your time and work, and kids will learn to do so too.

Madhavi is a qualified person, but stayed home to look after the kids. Now that her kids are fourteen and sixteen, she has taken up part-time work, so that they learn that their mother is not just to be taken for granted. However, this has not worked. Madhavi gets no co-operation at all, and now they leave the house even untidier and don't eat properly, since she is not in to supervise. They have no interest in what she does and never ask her what her day is like. The job is not well-paying, which is also something they joke about and tell her not to waste their time. Their father is extremely busy too and says that Madhavi should do what pleases her.

How do you get kids to appreciate that their mother too has a mind, some personal ambitions, and needs to be seen as a person and not just a comfort-provider?

Madhavi, it seems, wants validation and understanding from her kids as a primary point of her agenda, and follow her own pursuits and interests as a secondary part of her agenda. Perhaps she needs to be fully into what she is doing, without worrying about how this will 'teach the children' something. Simply taking up something to do to make a point will not work with teenagers.

A mother getting really involved with something that she likes to do, engrossed and contented with it, might gain genuine respect from her children for what she does. Teaching children to respect and appreciate a parent's 'me-time' starts much earlier than fourteen and sixteen. It is one of the healthiest things that you can do for yourself as well as your child. Once you're sure the kids are safe and looked after and occupied during the time that you are away (or even if you work on something out of home), going after your own pursuits is a great thing. A self-actualized parent, who is not constantly waiting on her children or worrying for them, or worse, feeling saintly for the career sacrifices that she has made, is a happier person. Working or pursuing interests that are yours alone is also a safety-valve from the constant pressure of responsible parenting.

Growing children, on their part, after some initial resistance, if any, learn to respect and appreciate that you are happy and occupied with something that you love to do. It also teaches them the value of having one's own pursuits and of allowing each other time and space.

After all, a parent who is there full-time for her or his child, but feels simmering frustration and resentment at the absence of any adult time to her or himself, might not be a great person to be around! The so-called sacrifice that parents make for their kids (by not pursuing any of their own interests), whether spelt out by the parent or implicit in her attitude, is something that weighs heavily on children, young and older. When younger, they don't quite know how to deal with parents' hurt and anger about them being ungrateful or unappreciative of what the parents say they 'sacrificed' for their kids. When older, they are bound to find the 'shrug' mechanism to deal with this litany.

Dos and Don'ts

- ❧ Teaching children to value your 'me-time' should start quite early. Thirteen to Fourteen years is a bit late.
- ❧ Be involved in something that you truly enjoy and chances are that your children will come around to respect you.
- ❧ Taking up a job or activity that you are productively engaged in is better than feeling resentful later about sacrificing a career.

Violence

Ignoring acts of small cruelty by kids and shielding their behaviour is one of the worst things a parent can do. It is essential to build a world of care and compassion within the family.

Parents who may have brought up their children to be considerate and compassionate often worry about having brash, insensitive, or spoilt kids in their immediate environment. How do we ensure that our child does not imbibe such attitudes from his or her peers?

Most of the unrepentant young people who you see today getting away with the most heinous crimes—from shooting someone over an argument, to driving recklessly over people are those whose parents have consistently not prevented them from acts of callousness, right from the smaller kind like torturing puppies, bullying other kids, and on to higher misdemeanours. And worse, they have protected and shielded them even when they have been caught at it. This goes under the name of 'parental love' or 'maa-baap ka pagal pyaar' and so on and so forth. How they have actually done a huge disservice to their children is something that seems to never sink in, even when they see their kids behind bars—in fact they continue to pretend to themselves and their kids that 'injustice' is being done or that their children are being 'victimized', and many such ridiculous postures and beliefs.

If, as a family you are compassionate and considerate to people, that's a big insurance against your child growing up to be a callous fiend. However, it is important that you also make an active statement about your attitudes. In the sense, taking a passive 'live and let live' stand is not enough anymore, given the level of callousness and brashness around us. Firstly, your kids must see you actively demonstrating qualities like considerateness, civic-mindedness, and a caring attitude. It is very well to be 'good people' in abstract terms when you do not have to deal with actual poor people, or get involved with their lives. So an important thing to add on to your family attitudes which may be currently right-thinking is also some active right-doing.

Remember, it is much easier for people to be callous to the poor when your life is not touched directly by poverty. The 'other' in any situation needs a face, close-up and personal—and that itself would make children immune to being drawn into some caper that involves endangering human lives and then laughing and paying their way out of their crimes. Free-floating and general compassion is fine, but it also needs an object of compassion—someone to be compassionate to. A further note of caution here: most people either teach their kids to ignore or distrust the poor, or to pity them. Neither are real or genuine positions. Pity doesn't stick. At best, it leads to the kind of guilt-ridden charity most of us suddenly do—giving away stuff (and worse, giving stuff we don't need in the first place!). Caring and compassion comes from giving. Which means, you need to expose your kids to (by way of actual interactions or at least in conversations and your own actions) people from lower strata in such a way that they can see some of the sterling qualities of people who are poor—not just see them as a pitiable mass of slaving-toiling sub-humans.

Secondly, you need to see that your kids take responsibility for the consequences of whatever they do. As one parent recently did, when she realized her son was part of a bunch of fifteen year-old-boys who strewed loads of scrap paper in one of their professor's garden: she got him to get back there next day and clean it up. Only two boys out of a bunch of eight were asked to do this by their parents.

Also, keep a close eye on what your kids' idea of fun is—especially if it involves cars and motorcycles, vandalism of any kind (even something as 'innocent' as stealing stuff from a five-star hotel toilet), and harassing women in any form. Often the 'boys will be boys' lazy-parenting syndrome ends up with boys becoming utter fools and later utterly dangerous fools.

Dos and Don'ts

- ❧ Never let your child get away with any kind of violence and cruelty to others. Take corrective action
- ❧ Be caring and compassionate yourself and be engaged in some active right doing, where you expose your kid to the lives of the poor and unprivileged, and emphasize some of their sterling qualities.
- ❧ Keep a check on what your kid's idea of fun is, and put an immediate stop to it if it is a nuisance in some form or the other.

Vocabulary

It is always a pleasure to listen to someone talk well in any language—someone with a good vocabulary, using it effectively. Kids can be encouraged to learn and understand a range of words, so that they become expressive and articulate them appropriately.

Dola says she finds her six-year-old at a loss for words many times. He wants to express himself, but his vocabulary is not good enough for it. Both she and his father are keen to see their son expand his vocabulary and enjoy using language to communicate well. He isn't shy, they say, he just does not have the words for many things and feelings.

Of course, a good vocabulary is not to be confused with the use of 'big words'. It is really the ability to use the right word for the right thing or feeling or thought. It is the ability to communicate well and to be able to articulate thoughts in such a way as to make them accessible to the listener.

Parents are so keen that their children develop a good vocabulary. Dictionaries are bought, 'meanings' mugged up, and kids are encouraged and goaded to read, read more—so as to improve their vocabulary. But an acquaintance with a large number of words is hardly a guarantee of good oral skills. And this is what we do, when we ask very young children mini-test questions like: Where is the fan? Show me something green…or worse, 'What's your name? Which school do you go to?'—when we already know the answer and the child knows that we know!

Why converse with a child as if life is a fill-in-the-blanks session? Surely, this is not how we talk during our normal day-to-day interactions. Fill-in-the-blank questions never lead to any real or actual conversation—stuff that makes for a good communicator. If you hold a real conversation—however tentative and faltering with a child, you are encouraging him to think, feel, *choose* words, form sentences, and to truly express. And you are also teaching him to listen. He then does not have to merely listen out for your question but engages in a conversation that involves absorbing ideas and generating his own response, even if it is at a very basic level. This is so much closer to the skills that he will actually need in the grown-up world, rather than the ability merely to label things right by plugging in the right word!

Of course, showing your child a ball and asking "What is this?" is one form of working on developing his/her vocabulary. But a much better way is to engage in conversation and to allow 'language to happen'. We enrich our children's vocabulary by enriching their lives. There are some key ways in which this can be done:

Don't hesitate to use all the right and 'grown-up' terms for something that the child enjoys. There's no need to 'dumb down' your language. For instance, if a child is fond of dogs, you can chat with her, however young she is, about what the dog eats, how you groom it, what games it plays, etc. without doing it in baby talk. This way a host of new words and concepts reach the child. She may not be able to use them immediately and appropriately, but the conversation is bound to open out a whole new toy box of terms for her—and children love that.

It is believed that children, from the time they learn to speak till the age of about six, learn at least twenty new words in a day. And this happens, not through vocabulary exercises and question-answer sessions. Children build their vocabulary by talking, reading, writing, and from *playing with words*. They begin to relish language play, even the interplay and punning between their mother tongue and English—an under three-year-old recently joked about going for a bath and eating bhaat (rice), much to his parents' delight. Kids take obvious delight in language—tell jokes, play word games, simply rhyme words, and move on to crosswords, creative, imaginative writing, etc. Do invest your time and energy in playing with words, sentences and ideas with your child.

The goal, then, should not be a strong vocabulary but a strong involvement with the world around them...the vocabulary will follow.

Dos and Don'ts

- An acquaintance with a large number of words is hardly a guarantee of good oral skills. Don't engage in mini-tests or fill-in-the-blanks kind of interactions all the time. Like what is your name...which class are you studying in... etc. It doesn't help develop conversational skills much.

- Use 'grown-up' terms and don't dumb down or baby talk with children. The kid may struggle with the conversation initially but the exercise will open a new world of words and concepts to her.

- Play with words, have games centered around it.

W for

War-cries

❧

Siblings snarling and scratching each other are performing a rite of passage. While parents need to intervene if any serious damage is being inflicted, broadly it is a good idea to refuse to play referee each time.

Gayatri says that her two kids have been constantly fighting since her daughter has turned eight and her son twelve. If it's not an all-out war, it's arguing or bickering. They constantly approach the parents to intervene, take sides, reprimand the other one, or just to complain. They barely manage 15 minutes together before one runs back to complain, making it impossible for Gayatri to get any work done. Both parents want to find ways for the kids to fight less and to sort out their own issues. They are even considering sending one off to a boarding school.

Ever seen a pair of puppies on the roadside? Or tiger cubs on Discovery? They're playing, snarling, tumbling, bullying, nipping, and fighting over some piece of food, all day long. It's the socialization process! So firstly, it doesn't seem like a good idea to split the kids up—they need to do what they're doing.

Though the fist-fest that parents like Gayatri witness everyday may not seem like it, a whole lot of emotional and social processes are being put in place during this time, quite naturally, and at an early stage: sharing of parental love and attention, developing patience, dealing with irrationality or unfairness, caring and responsibility, and other such issues. Many corners are rounded off during the growing years, consciously as well as unconsciously. This prepares children later on in their lives to deal with the outside adult world of co-operative living, teamwork, sharing of resources, relationship building, social skills, putting up with idiosyncrasies, etc.

However, it can be quite trying to constantly play referee and third umpire during these friendly and not-so-friendly matches, so parents in this situation could try one simple device, that one parent has honed to perfection: 'go deaf' and 'become invisible' the minute they come up to you for arbitration and intervention! Simply refuse to engage. Get involved only if there is any chance of serious physical damage to life, limb or property (which a fight between two boys can quickly escalate to). For bickering, name-calling, grabbing space and stuff, arguing over what to play and who said what to whom, become totally unavailable. One overwrought parent even resorted to telling her kids calmly (and frustratingly): 'Don't tell me; come I'll drive you to the police station and you can put in your complaint there'. A few such innovative, even outlandish non-engaging replies and you can hope for them to not just stop-it-at-once but even enjoy watching them giggling and the whole fight fizzling out.

Many parents report that their similarly snarly-scratchy kids become sweet and supportive of each other when the parents are out of the house or when they go to stay over at a friend's or relative's place without the parents. This means that you as a parent constitute an 'audience' to these WWF wrestling bouts and courtroom dramas. Find ways not to witness them at all—don't keep an ear out for rising voices, and leave the room if something erupts, or play deaf and at times invisible.

Dos and Don'ts

- As much as possible, go 'invisible' and 'deaf' when the warring siblings come to you for intervention. Only engage if you sense a physical damage to life, limb or property.
- If at all, give innovative, outlandish replies, which will make a joke of the whole thing and cool tempers immediately.
- Kids fight to gain attention. When you refuse to accord it any importance, the siblings will learn to cohabit better.
- Don't be overly anxious about the fights. Many corners are rounded off during the growing years, consciously as well as unconsciously. This prepares children to deal later with the outside adult world of co-operative living.

Whereabouts

Youngsters need to let their parents know where they are and how they can be contacted. This is not a nosy-parent trick, but something that works towards their own safety, and it is important that they accept this.

Jeannie shares a good rapport with her fifteen-year-old daughter Ava. However, the daughter has been recently asking, half-jokingly, if her mom too, is going to 'grill' her with questions when next year, in Junior College, she gets to go out on her own with friends. Jeannie has told her that there will of course be some negotiating of the line between Ava's freedom and privacy. It's a tough call for parents, when their kids are growing, to decide what things are important to know and what things can remain unasked.

Parents ask questions that may appear nosy to young teens, but those who, like Jeannie, have a good rapport with their child, perhaps could come up with the areas that are 'legit'—where you can legitimately ask for information—and areas you need to not know about. Firstly make it clear that what appears nosy, are really questions whose answers will define whether your child is going to be safe or not when he or she goes out on her own. Safety—physical and emotional—is an issue, and can't be just dismissed as your 'needless worrying' or 'interference'.

These are legitimate questions, to which you can reasonably expect clear replies:

Where are you going? From this the parent back at home knows how far from home is the area that is their destination and the route to this place. You could suggest better ways of getting there if there are any potentially dodgy areas that they have to negotiate.

What will you be doing? Here you can figure out if they're doing healthy, 'normal' things, and if someone in the group has some other ideas that are potentially dangerous or illegal or unsavoury in any way.

When will you come back? Rather than a question, this should be a time that you set which is realistic as well as safe. This should not be negotiable; stick with what you think is the right time to get back home.

Who is with you? You definitely need to know how many people are going to be there, and who all they are. Reserve your comments on whether you like all of these people or not, if they are not troublemakers. Be prepared not to like all of her friends. If there's anyone in the group who is known to be reckless or a bit on the wild side, you can indicate that your daughter need not follow any sudden changes of program that this person may suggest.

How are you going and how are you getting back? A fair enough question—it will help your daughter pre-plan safe and sensible ways to get back home in time and without any odd encounters.

You could impress upon your child the fact that lying about any of these questions could put her and her friends in some serious trouble that they may not have anticipated; moreover, once they lie about any of this, it is difficult for them to quickly seek out help if anything goes wrong, because they then worry about their lie getting exposed. 'It's just not worth lying about these things' is what your child needs to learn.

Dos and Don'ts

- ❧ Your teenager might consider your questions nosy but mark out some legit areas where you can seek answers any time.
- ❧ Stress that you are asking questions to ensure her safety and nothing else.
- ❧ Give her some useful suggestions based on her responses, so that it remains at the back of her mind.
- ❧ Discourage her from lying, as that would make it difficult to seek out help if suddenly something goes wrong.

Y for

Yelling

❧

Shouting and screaming at a baby or toddler comes from a mother who is either exhausted, needs support, or is emotionally unbalanced. Anyone who wants to intervene should do so with sensitivity and with solutions.

A young overworked mother, Masooma has been told by several friends and relatives that she is shouting far too much at her eighteen-month-old. She yells at him when he does typical baby things like grabbing everything in sight or pulling other kids' hair. She also uses negative language in front of him like calling him 'stupid' or 'senseless.' When anyone brings it up with her, Masooma's explanation is that different people use different parenting techniques! Her friend Roma really wants to intervene and save both the mother and child from getting into an ugly dysfunctional scenario.

While it is difficult to intervene in matters of this sort, as her friend, Roma could try to figure out what is at work, and then offer support or advice. It's best to tackle this kind of thing—any criticism of someone's parenting—by weaving in an alternative or a suggestion about how to do things differently. This way the parent neither gets on the defensive nor feels helpless. As a friend, she could observe and intervene kindly but quickly—because, however much one may understand where the yelling is coming from, Roma has to work to getting Masooma to stop yelling at her child; it must be damaging the child every time, for sure. And something like this can only escalate if she isn't helped.

Here's what could be happening: Almost every mother at some time is distraught and may resort to yelling. But usually she will be sufficiently shocked at herself to find other ways of coping. This happens usually by her recognizing that she is tired and strung-out, hungry or sleepy or in desperate need of some non-child related interactions with other adults. She will then find a friend, relative, or her spouse to takeover for a while and give her some time away from the infant or baby a relaxing experience. So if you think this is what's happening, you could gently put it to her that she is stressed out and needs to work with some breaks. She needs to get some time to herself with the co-operation of her spouse or other empathetic friends or relatives. This way, Roma can introduce the idea to this stressed mother that her yelling and angry words are not appropriate. At the same time, Roma can offer understanding as well as some kind of a solution together with her criticism of Masooma's behaviour with her baby.

The other thing that could be operating might be that Masooma is a person with serious anger issues herself, and needs to tackle them. The words she uses, like 'stupid' and 'senseless' seem to point in that direction too. Observe if this is part of her general behaviour—being angry and dismissive and hyper-critical of herself and her world. Now this is something difficult to put to anyone at a friendly level, but if this is what is at work, you could say it out to her one day, not when she is not letting fly at her child, but when you can have a chat.

The third thing that Roma would need to figure out is whether the child is hyperactive and some kind of investigation is needed on that front. It would be best to check with the father or any other adult who interacts with the child, to see if he is really difficult to cope with. There too, a concerned friend can suggest that she should go see a good pediatrician.

The bottom line of course is that no one should yell at a powerless child, and definitely not use angry adult words.

Dos and Don'ts

- Try offering an alternative to a friend whose ways of parenting you do not approve of, rather than criticizing her.
- The reason many mothers lose their temper or yell is out of frustration. Often, they are just desperate for some adult company and non-child interaction. Let her know she is stressed and encourage her to take a break.
- Investigate if the child is hyperactive and is the cause of the strain.

Z for

Zzztime

When is it time for a child to move to her own bed and possibly own bedroom? It's a difficult transition if your child has been in your bedroom for all of his or her early years.

Uma's seven-year-old daughter likes to sleep with her parents. They have got a new bed for her, and even done up her room, but she refuses to sleep in the bed at night. She has slept with her parents' from the very beginning. They have now managed to convince her to sleep in her bed during the day but want to switch this to the night time too. They are confused because some of their friends say a child should never be forced to sleep elsewhere unless she wants to herself.

The world, it seems, is sharply divided between people who think its fine to have kids in their bed till they're ready for their own room; and those who think it's a complete no-no and is to be discouraged from as early as possible. This is a parenting poser that is fiercely debated by psychologists, families, doctors, parents, and kids.

A whole lot of parents in India, even urban Indians with Westernized lifestyles, do accommodate their kids in their rooms, their beds, up to the age of even thirteen and fourteen. They're not too sure it's the right thing—because it clearly prevents parents from having, not just sex and intimacy in the bedroom at night, but even plain adult conversations, not meant for kids to participate in. But they allow it anyway.

Let's first look at why a kid prefers to sleep with you, and why you hesitate to firmly shut her out. The primary reason is that we are told that children grow up more secure this way. That to my mind, is a debatable issue in the first place. Your child doesn't need to share your bed to be secure and happy. And more importantly, sleeping with parents is no guarantee against insecurities; moreover, their fears need to be and can be dealt with in other ways. Then there is the sheer discomfort of poking knees and butting heads. All in all, no one gets rest, most of the times.

Secondly, many of us in India tend to either not acknowledge or not give adequate weight to the adult man-woman relationship, once we become parents. There is often a guilt attached in spelling out to children that you need your own space and time, with yourself and with your spouse. So it seems more convenient to, by default, let all sleep in the same space.

One grave danger of this is that our children have very poorly etched ideas about what their parents' relationship is like, and to accept and be equanimous with the fact that their parents have a relationship with each other at certain levels which do not include them. This, to my mind, is clearly an impediment in a child's development and transition into young adulthood. (That one spouse finds it 'convenient' to insert a kid into the marital bed, so that intimacy can be avoided, is also a factor at work—but then that is a whole other set of issues.)

Once they're in the habit, it's difficult to get kids to sleep elsewhere. In spite of whatever way you 'dress it up', the kid feels that she is being banished. The bottom line is that every parent has to decide if you want this enough—your own space for the night. And then do what it takes—ranging from mild cajoling, rewards and explanations, preferably starting by the age of three or four. You could begin by being in the child's new room for a while—the child put to bed, and you reading (to her) or for yourself, chatting with your spouse in a low voice, with the clear understanding that you will exit to your room in half an hour. There is bound to be some crying and protest, but if you really want it, you'll find a way.

Dos and Don'ts

- Value your adult man-woman relationship and don't sacrifice it at the altar of parenthood. Do not compromise on private time with your spouse.
- Start getting your child to sleep separately from the age of three or four years. Coax, cajole, or reward her—do what it takes.
- If she is still unwilling, spend some time with her in her room, read to her or to yourself, and then find a way to your own bedroom.

A couple having sex with a small child fast asleep in the same room—not uncommon in India, and yet is highly unadvisable since it causes parents to feel strapped in time and space for intimacy and their need to find different solutions.

Mrs Ganguly is the mother of a sixteen-month- old child. As she and her husband do not have a separate cot or room for their son, he sleeps with them in the same bed. Mr and Mrs Ganguly generally make love after he has slept but there are times, she says, that he does wake up and stares at them or begins to cry. This has affected their sex life and they have fights over this, as the husband feels that they could attempt to have sex by keeping some bolsters or some other visual block between them and the child. She feels that this too would be inappropriate. How do couples deal with this situation?

Many parents confidently state about this issue: "They don't understand anything till they are older". However, this seems only a convenient assumption that 'babies don't register such things'. It is a well established fact that babies do register a lot.

Firstly, this situation needs to be something that both parents should address together. Many men are impatient with their wife's hesitation on this front, and take it as a personal slight and rejection. Perhaps it is time to grow up, now that he is not just a husband but a father too.

Many grown-up people who as babies had witnessed their parents having sex, simply could not process what they witnessed. It has usually led to a deep-rooted fear/anger/ disgust with one or the other parent.

An important point here is, if the parents are planning to be open and easy about the body, nudity, talk about sex, demonstrating physical affection between husband and wife etc. in their future life with their child, there is some (vague) justification for having sex in the room just now. However, most Indian families are so very puritanical and unwilling to be easy about any of those things, that a child then finds it even more difficult to process what he or she has seen in the bedroom between the parents in his or her early years.

Of course in our overflowing country, with its cramped living conditions in most places, many children per force witness the sexual act in some form at some time. However, since Mrs Ganguly is well aware that this could be a problem, and is also increasingly uncomfortable with it, they, as a couple, need to explore other options. To start with, the baby could be given a small cot or cradle. The couple could also think of other places in the house to use. Going away on a weekend together, and leaving the baby with a grandparent or aunt or some other family member, so that they can be fully available physically and emotionally to each other for a bit outside of the home situation and certainly away from the baby is another possibility that young parents could explore in trying to maintain a sex life for themselves.

Dos and Don'ts

- If you do not have a separate room for the kid, arrange for a separate cot or cradle.
- Take weekends off, dropping the child at a family member's place, so you can be fully available—physically and emotionally—to each other.

Acknowledgements

Some of the material for this book came from my long-running column, Learning Curve, with the HT-Media paper, *Mint*. I thank Priya Ramani and Seema Chowdhry of *Mint*, and reader-parents of the paper for the platform that they provide for important parenting issues to be aired and tackled.

Thank you Kanishka Gupta, of Writersside, for his enthusiasm, patience, and that combination of simplicity and the smarts!

Thank you to my friend and reader-reviewer Sandhya Iyer for reading through and wording the section intros.

Thank you to all the children, teenagers, young adults, and parents who have trusted me with their troubles, have worked hard during the counselling process, have passed through the tunnel, turned around and waved from the bright other side, to tell me that they are doing okay!

Gratitude and affection for Dr Minnu and Rajan Bhonsle, trainers, friends, enablers. Thank you to Dr Dayal Mirchandani, for your training and thought-provoking lessons.

Thank you to the late Dr Ashok Ranade—thinker, musician, academic, family-friend—who urged me to write on parenting.

I owe much to Jaya, who continues to throw me parenting challenges as well as love in equal measure.

A Note on the Author

Gouri Dange is a writer and practising family counsellor based in Pune and Mumbai, India. Her columns, features, and fiction appear in magazines, newspapers and anthologies as well as on social media sites. In her counselling as well as in her writing, she is particularly interested in the human ability to grow and develop, as well as the equally human tendency to resist growth and change. She is the author of three novels—*3 Zakia Mansion*, *The Counsel of Strangers*, and *Viva Voce,* and has previously published a book on parenting—*ABCs of Parenting*.

Gouri Dange can be contacted at write2gouri@gmail.com.